CONTENTS

UNFINISHED	5
FORWARD	6
THE OPEN DOOR	7
A PENNY FOR YOUR THOUGHTS	13
HOMECOMING	17
NICE TO MEET YOU	21
THAT SUMMER	25
WHERE ARE YOU?	28
JULY 10, 1964	32
DAVE'S GONE	33
HE CAN'T BE HERE	38
DEJA VUE	41
IS THIS ALL THERE IS?	45
ON THE ROCKS	48
OVER THE CLIFF...ER...EDGE	52
IF IT'S TOO GOOD TO BE TRUE	60
A PRIVATE HELL	67
WIDE OPEN SPACES	72
TRAPPED	77
ON THE ROAD AGAIN	84
LIFE AS A GHOST HUNTER	89

THE MANUSCRIPT	94
IS IT REALLY YOU?	98
THE READING	104
MEMORY LANE	111
LETTER TO DAVE	121
A LIGHT ON THE SUBJECT	124
LETTER TO DAVE	128
THE HEADSTONE	130
LETTER TO DAVE	132
THE GREATER GOOD	134
LETTER TO DAVE	137
KEEP YOUR EYES OPEN GIRL	138
LETTER TO DAVE	141
THAT FIRST INVESTIGATION	142
LETTER TO DAVE	145
WHO ARE YOU?	146
LETTER TO DAVE	151
PAST LIVES	153
LETTER TO DAVE	160
VISION vs. DNA	162
LETTER TO DAVE	165
A BIRTHDAY GIFT	166
LETTER TO DAVE	168
THE BATTLEFIELD INVESTIGATION	169
LETTER TO DAVE	172
A MOVING TARGET	174
LETTER TO DAVE	176
WHERE ARE THEY?	178

LETTER TO DAVE	181
A DISAPPEARING ACT	183
LETTER TO DAVE	185
A NORMAL LIFE	187
LETTER TO DAVE	189
GOODBYE?	191
LETTER TO DAVE	194
DOUBTS	196
LETTER TO DAVE	198
DEAR DAVE	200
THAT IS THE QUESTION	205
THE NOW	208
AFTERWARD	211
ABOUT THE AUTHOR	213

UNFINISHED

In This Life and the Next

Carol Martindale-Taylor

FORWARD

When you deny emotional pain, everything you do or think as well as your relationships, become contaminated with it.

Eckart Tolle in 'Practicing the Power of Now,' 1999

THE OPEN DOOR

Easing down on the twin mattress, the icy sheet sucked the breath out of me. With no other option for my cold feet, I snuggled down in a pile of blankets and waited for my own body heat to bring relief. Rolling onto my left side, I tugged the bundled mass up under my chin.

The blankets bunched up over my right hip pushed down against me, the sensation snaking across my lower back to my left hip.

What the...oh, oh. Dave?

It was early 2014, and as a Lead Investigator in a paranormal team, I still struggled with my belief that such phenomena happened to others, but would never happen to me. That was just one of many mistakes I made over the years.

When Dave, my first real love, died in 1964, I understood it to be permanent. I went on to marry, graduate from college, travel —all things one does in life, but with one caveat. I unknowingly kept my survivor's guilt well satisfied for the next five decades.

Saving other men became a quest, explaining my life-long choice in partners. If they were emotionally and financially secure, I was not interested in them beyond friendship. It was not until I re-read my short story about losing Dave that unhealed wounds surfaced and my epiphany roared overhead.

Damn it, that's what I've done! I didn't save him, so I found other men to save.

Well, I can't blame him for what happened. I did that myself, but at least now I know why—and he knows how I love it when he tucks me in at night.

Fifty years in the making, ours is a story of love and healing coming from the Other Side.

***

"Hey, how about I bring a friend over one night? His name's Dave, he's 19, and he's the coxswain on the captain's gig for the *USS Mahan*."

Bob's brotherly frustration had long since zipped past its boiling point. After graduation from high school in 1960, he joined the Navy and started a long distance relationship with Alice, one of my best friends. After she and I graduated from the same school in Iowa the next year, my parents and I moved to San Diego where Bob and I developed a close friendship.

"Sure," I said without hesitation, "but I'll have to tell him about Rich."

A Marine stationed in Twentynine Palms, Rich sporadically visited me and stayed with my parents. My very first steady boyfriend, it took time to realize I did not have to put up with accusations of a lesbian relationship because I said "no" to sex, or his tales of former girlfriends. My creative piece of writing telling him he could still visit, but I would date others, was already in his hands.

"That's okay," Bob responded. "I think Dave's sort of involved with somebody back home in Georgia, but it's nothing serious."

On Friday night, May 24 of 1963, Bob brought James David Alligood into my life.

Average height and average build, nothing else was average about him. His wavy hair, hazel eyes embedded with green flecks, and handsome features did not fascinate me. His low-keyed manner did. Rich was a boy. Dave was a young man.

"By the way," I interrupted during a break in our conversation, "I've been seeing a Marine from Twentynine Palms. We're not really a couple, but he comes to town on weekends sometimes, and stays here."

For the first time I heard Dave's soft, amused chuckle.

"That's okay. There's a girl back in Georgia I've been seeing. We're not engaged or anything, although Lisa has been pushing for a ring. Pushing a little too hard actually." His voice trailed off as his gaze shifted to our hardwood floor.

So began our magic with no jealousies, no expectations, and no demands. We slipped into a relationship without fanfare, understanding what it was, if not where it was going. I would continue dating Rich, Dave would continue his long-distance relationship with Lisa, and we would date others.

I mailed Rich a letter about a sailor walking into my life, but Dave and I never discussed it or how he handled Lisa.

***

The city bus became Dave's best friend on date nights until I began picking him up Saturday mornings. Ever the gentleman, after returning him to the Seven Seas Locker Club Sunday evenings, he always watched until my lumbering white Mercury safely pulled away from the curb before he went inside to change into his uniform and return to the *Mahan*.

Those dates revealed something else about Dave—young women flirted with him in front of me. A master at ignoring them, at least when I was present, I thankfully never felt threatened as I so often did when Rich ranted about his girlfriends.

Maybe women were fascinated by Dave's twinkling eyes, or cute smile with its chipped front tooth, a souvenir from plowing face down on the pavement when he wrecked his Chevy. Maybe his Georgia drawl attracted them, or maybe his bad boy image seeped through. He did confess that by the time he enlisted in the Navy, the nice girls back home were being warned not to date him.

On our first quiet evening at home, we excused ourselves and I led him to my parent's sitting room. I snuggled up against him in the dark, tingling with the warmth of his touch as his arm wrapped around my shoulders. Kissing the hollow of his neck and lost in the deep, sweet scent of Old Spice aftershave lotion, he hugged me when my contented sigh escaped. I was home.

After weekends of exploring touches, his patience proved

staggering when I still said "no" to sex. Even at 20 years old, my fear of an unwed pregnancy breaking my parent's heart never failed to put on the brakes.

"I have never seen anyone so ready and still say no," he whispered one night, kissing my cheek. It was the only comment he ever made about sex. He never criticized me or made me feel guilty, and he never, ever left me feeling unloved.

And so June and early July passed with us lost in a relationship growing without words of love. Lost that was, until I received a letter from Alice.

Walking back from the mail box suspended outside our front door, I stopped in the middle of the living room.

"Hey, Alice wants to know if she can move in with us for a few weeks. She wants to look for a job and an apartment here so she can be close to Bob."

My parents shared one of those looks, the kind a couple married over 20 years exchange, then nodded yes in unison.

"Sure," came from my mother.

"You know, if she comes out here, the thing to do would be for the two of us to get an apartment together." I watched her reaction.

The year before, talk of trying apartment living with a co-worker at the American Automobile Association caused such angst, I dropped the subject. My argument against "nice girls live at home until they get married," consisted of "I can do anything in the backseat of a car that I can do in an apartment." It fell on deaf ears.

Maybe she did not want another round of arguments with me or my father over the subject.

"Okay, but be careful what neighborhood you move into, and don't go getting into something you can't afford."

"Yes, mother."

I rolled my eyes at my father.

***

Alice's arrival created such a fun foursome, I forgot about the *Mahan's* departure for its seven-month cruise across the Western Pacific.

"You know the ship leaves for WestPac on August 6," Dave whispered. I was in the middle of delivering a shower of kisses to his left ear.

"Oh, that's right." My last kiss went undelivered. I slumped back against the sofa.

"And Lisa's flying out here next weekend," he reminded me.

"So I guess this weekend is our last for a while."

"We can still go out Friday night."

"Okay, that works."

End of discussion.

It was time for me to disappear, as Dave did when Rich visited one weekend. Lisa would fly into San Diego on Saturday, July 27, and spend the week with him before the ship set sail.

That Friday night, we stayed home for a quiet goodbye.

"The *Mahan*'ll be back in early March, so I'll see you then."

"Sounds good," I whispered.

Getting up from our now favorite sofa, we headed for the front door. Stopping in the hallway, he reached into his back pants pocket for his wallet, then held something out to me.

"Here. I just had this taken."

"Thanks." Glancing down at his professional photograph, I smiled. "Hey, I've never seen you in uniform before."

"Hopefully, you won't again either," he laughed. Resting his hand in my small of my back, he guided me to the front door.

"Listen, you don't need to drive me to the Locker Club tonight. I'll take the bus back."

"Are you sure? I don't mind driving you downtown."

"I'm sure." It was a final decision.

Opening the door, he turned back and kissed my cheek. Walking out into the blackest of San Diego nights, his silhouette crossed our road under a street light and disappeared.

I closed the door behind him.

***

"Carol, it's Dave," my mother called out from the living room.

Taking his telephone call on our kitchen wall phone, my

"hello" was more of a question than a greeting.

"Hi. Listen, Lisa's on a plane back to Georgia. Is there any chance we can get together before I leave?" His soothing Southern drawl flowed.

"Sure. When?"

"I have duty Saturday, so maybe Sunday."

"Okay. Bob's taking Alice sightseeing Sunday, and they've invited me along. I'm sure we can make it a foursome."

"That works. I'll talk to Bob, okay?"

"Yeah."

"See you then. Bye."

"Bye."

I stared at the receiver clutched in my hand.

It's only Tuesday. Why is Lisa already on a plane back to Georgia?

Deemed too wild for the daughters of some, that Dave would have let Lisa stay with him all week and kept me waiting in the wings. Not this Dave.

I asked no questions, he volunteered no explanations, and nothing felt more natural.

A PENNY FOR YOUR THOUGHTS

Driving through a dense morning fog on Sunday, Bob's car nosed westward along Interstate 8, then north up Old Highway 101. Taking a side street, we twisted along the narrow road until finding a parallel parking slot. Sliding out of our seats as the sun won its battle against the mist, we walked a few steps to the lookout point.

The outcrop dropped straight down to a deserted beige beach below us, incoming waves rushing headlong in search of sand.

We became part of the scenery in front of a hazy bluff squeezed between dark green California scrubs and a pencil thin string of buildings. The broken horizon stretched far to our west, with the bluff giving up the last of its land to the Point Loma Lighthouse.

Dave released my hand and left me standing with Alice and Bob. Creating a path down the cliff face, he reached a level patch of ground beneath us where he stood hands on hips, staring into a placid Pacific Ocean.

I studied him from above.

I wish I had a penny for your thoughts. Are you questioning what you've done?

Reaching some unspoken decision, he spun around and climbed back up the embankment. Stopping in mid stride when our eyes met, he smiled that smile, and pulled me to him as he crested the top.

Bob shattered our brief magical moment.

"Hey, over here," he yelled loud enough to draw the ire of bystanders as his camera clicked. Laughing over our broken spell, we joined Alice and Bob as they headed back to the car.

"And for our next tourist attraction," Bob announced, taking Alice's hand, "let's go to Mission de Alcala."

***

The noon sun bore down as we drove east toward Mission de Alcala, each mile putting another exclusive hotel behind us. So typical of a coastal summer day, the farther inland we went, the higher the temperature, the bluer the sky, and the drier the air. Air conditioning meant lowering car windows until you arrive at a cooler destination.

Hidden from view, the 1769 mission rests on the north side of Mission Valley and is invisible unless you know where to look. Working our way off the highway and through trees greened by remnants of long lost river drainage, we found its parking lot.

Rushing through a side entrance of the cool adobe building, we found ourselves in a lush garden secreted away in an interior patio. Making our way to the gift shop, Alice and I picked out brochures explaining the self-guided walking tour, while Dave looked through postcards and Bob watched the female clerk flirt with him.

Finding our way out of the shop, tightly trimmed hedges bordering a rainbow of flowers showered us with the scent of lavender. We strolled past religious statues framed by the purple crepe-paper flowers of bougainvillea, and grassy edges hugging golden hibiscus. Guided along a path through breezy halls flanked by sandstone archways, we worked our way through gloomy dorm rooms where two monks slept who were killed during a Native American uprising.

Holding hands as we watched ceramic tiles pass beneath our feet, Dave and I bumped into our friends. Laughing, they directed our gaze up to the twisted trunks of centuries-old olive trees ahead of us. The gray, grotesque shapes left over from some Halloween horror show, provided only a temporary distraction.

Subdued, occasionally teasing, Dave released my hand, putting his arm around me. There was no talk of Lisa, or Rich, or the coming months.

Satisfied we captured all the historic mission had to offer, we wandered outside, squinting against a glaring sun.

Heat waves rippled over cement covering the ancient red bricks beneath us as we worked our way to the front of the mission. Years of sun worshiping stripped away the front door's brown stain and cracked sections of the outer adobe wall covering. Broken slabs laid bare the narrow, uneven brickwork underneath, exposing the mission's original facade.

"Hey, this is a great place for pictures." Alice, stepping aside, pulled a camera out of her handbag. Mindlessly following her lead, I reached for mine as the two guys jostled for positions on the front steps to pose for us.

Three of us missed the flash of color bouncing past our feet. Dave did not. Snatching up the little calico kitten, he cradled her in his right arm while we snapped pictures. Clawing out her release, she scrambled off, making him forget his chipped front tooth long enough to laugh out loud.

"Go ahead, you two stand there and I'll get some pictures," Alice instructed me, readying her Kodak.

As I replaced Bob, Dave took my hand and turned me toward him.

Our eyes held each other for one brief second before Bob struck again.

"Hey, it's about that time," he called out, breaking another spell. "We need to finish up here and get downtown." He nodded toward a brilliant disk on its downward swing west of us.

Posing for official pictures after that proved impossible. Through tear-filled laughter, Dave and I play fought over whose outfit went best with my white handbag.

By the time we arrived downtown, the Seven Seas Locker

Club glowed orange.

"Well, the ship sails at 9:00 a.m. Tuesday." Dave's soft voice broke the silence.

"Okay, I'll take off work that morning. Will you leave from 32nd Street?"

"Yeah, but I probably won't be able to talk to you."

"That's okay."

"Sounds good," he sighed. "I'll write and let you know how things go."

"Not too much about how things go."

He chuckled, knowing how I felt about prostitutes in ports of call—just don't tell me.

"Bye you guys." He looked up at Alice and Bob in the front seat. "See you in March."

"Yep, see you in March," Bob repeated.

Giving me a quick kiss, Dave slid out of the backseat, and walked into the Club.

***

On the cloudless morning of August 6, 1963, the small crowd on the 32nd Street Pier ignored the punishing sun. Everyone stared in the same direction, some with tears streaming down their faces, some helping infants raise chubby hands to wave goodbye.

Look at all of them hanging over the railings. I'll never find him.

In my favorite blue and green silk print dress, skirt billowing in an onshore breeze, I searched faces until the ship began its pull away from the pier.

I'll bet he sees me though.

The sleek, metallic gray *Mahan* slipped out of the turquoise sky and dipped below the horizon.

HOMECOMING

Alice and I soon moved into our own apartment, and with extra time on our hands, plunged into volunteer work and night classes. Then we heard from Sande, another close friend from our graduating class.

She and her high school boyfriend broke up after he left for college, so she too wanted to try life in Southern California. We invited her to join us—three good friends and rent split three ways was too good to pass up. Alice and I moved into our master bedroom, and Sande took up residence in our smaller second bedroom.

It did not take long for a quagmire to rear its ugly little head. Three women sharing living quarters can pit two against one if problems creep into the mix, and creep they did. Aside from believing Sande ignored her share of the cleaning chores around the apartment, we stewed over her handling of Rich's friend in the Marine Corps.

Having met Sande on her previous visit to California, he began making the trek from Twentynine Palms with Rich to date her, and staying at my parent's house. It worked well until someone else caught Sande's eye. Her boss.

Alice and I, deciding it was none of our business, hoped the problem would go away if we ignored it long enough.

***

Over San Diego's version of winter, Bob introduced me to another sailor. Johnny and I developed the kind of friendship that would be there when I needed it most.

In the meantime, President Kennedy's assassination, the *Mahan* cruising near some unknown place called Vietnam, and a sailor far ahead of his time who was found sniffing glue onboard the ship, were the subjects of letters between Dave and myself. Rich, Lisa, and the future were on their own.

I mailed Dave copies of the pictures taken the Sunday before he left, and he sent Polaroid pictures of him in his work clothes and one taken after a fight. The impressive swollen nose and cut over his left eye introduced someone I had yet to meet.

Who was this person who became so enraged, he got into a fight?

***

With Rich turning 21 on the first Saturday in March, I helped him celebrate at my parent's house, but my mind was elsewhere. As soon as he left, I dashed home.

Dave's coming home Tuesday. I've got to figure out what to wear!

On another clear morning two days later, Alice and I met the *Mahan* as it plowed back into San Diego Harbor. This time, the pier was packed by a more jubilant crowd than the one sending it off the previous August.

Concentrating on faces coming off the ship, I flinched when a sailor in dress whites popped up in front of me. A quick kiss, that grin, and Dave was back in my life.

Escorted on a tour of the ship, we found Christmas in March. He brought home a stereo console and musical jewelry box for me, a china tea service for my mother, and even a gift for Alice so she would not feel left out. For himself, he bought a good Seiko wristwatch and two tailor-made cashmere suits.

Suits?

Why not a dressy dinner to celebrate his return? Alice and I begged the use of my parent's house—needing a kitchen counter longer than a toaster—and invited Dave and Bob to a special party.

***

"Hi boys, come on in." Stepping aside to close the door behind our guests, my father turned around to call for us. Already there, I stared.

Black cashmere suit, white dress shirt, tie, cuff links.
Wow...

Dave eyed my rose colored street-length gown, long dark hair pulled back in a French twist, and dangling pearl earrings. He did not need to say a word.

"Okay everybody, before you get comfortable, let me take a picture." My father motioned us toward the front door for a backdrop.

In the few seconds it took to pose, I slid my left hand behind Dave where his right hand wrapped around it. We never could be close and not touch.

"Okay, that's it." My father retreated, leaving the four of us waiting on a roast still roasting.

"I have to tell you what happened with some of the guys," Dave began as we settled into an assortment of living room chairs.

"When we were in port, one of them ended up in a place that got raided by the police, so he panicked and dove out a window. Problem was, he forgot he was on the second floor until he landed in the bushes below!"

The visual brought a round of laughter.

"One of the other guys made a quick trip back home as soon as we got here, and he's back now with a disease he thinks he caught from his girlfriend. She was a virgin when he left."

"Oh no!" Bob's comment brought out a sympathetic reaction around the room.

"And another one got married before we left because his girlfriend didn't want to worry about him being faithful to her while he was gone."

Before we finished mulling over her logic, he spoke up again. "Me? I bragged about how I don't have to lie about what I did over there."

His smile surrounded me.

How I loved knowing he felt no need to lie to me. He never

offered details as I knew he would not, and as I am sure he expected, I never questioned him. He was a 20-year-old single young man, and it was only paid-for sex.

"Hey girls, I think your roast is ready," my mother called out from the kitchen.

Running for aprons, Alice and I went back to creating our picture perfect dinner, aided by my mother's pecan pie so loved by Dave. Minutes later, returning to the living room to announce dinner, my mother's comment gave me an idea.

"Hey Dave, did you let your mother know you made it back to San Diego okay?"

"No, I didn't." His response was slow as he looked up at me from an armchair.

No man ever looked at me the way he did right then. Not before, not since. Love, and amusement, and "damn, I want to get you in bed," rolled into one glance.

"You know, she might be worried. Mom said it's okay if you want to call her from here."

"Yeah, I probably should."

He headed for the spare bedroom telephone, while the rest of us worked out who was sitting where around the dining room table.

"Yeah, she was glad to hear from me," he said a few minutes later, pulling out the chair next to me.

I wonder if she knows about me?

"Okay, everybody for themselves." Alice waved her hand over steaming dishes and icy drinks.

NICE TO MEET YOU

The following Saturday, my mother talked with Dave while rummaging around the kitchen putting our lunch together. A light, balmy day, I used my father as an excuse to go outside where he worked on a stubborn patch of crabgrass in the backyard.

"Hey Dad, lunch is almost ready."

"Good, I'm about done here," he called over his shoulder.

"What do you want on your sand..."

"Hello," a voice called out from the back porch.

Oh no!

My father, turning to look over my head, struggled to keep a straight face.

"Hi," he called out, a rake bouncing on his shoulder as he walked toward the tool shed. Even from the side, I could see his grin giving way to a full-blown smile.

What do I do?

"Ah, hi Rich. What are you doing here?" came out of me when I managed to look in his direction.

That sounded crass.

"I thought I told you about my discharge. Anyway, I wanted to see you before I leave Friday."

Whew...oh, no! Where's Dave?

My mother said they introduced themselves to each other in the living room, then Rich went out the back door and Dave the front.

Did I tell Rich it was nice knowing him before his friends picked him up the next morning? My best guess is yes.

I wonder what he would have said if he hadn't run into Dave?

Rich's visit prompted another Tuesday evening telephone call from Dave, with another light laugh.

"You should have seen the look on his face," was his only comment.

It was Dave's turn to not question, and mine to not volunteer.

***

The week of my 21st birthday, the *Mahan* cruised the local reaches of the Pacific while I overlooked the same stretch of water with Dave's birthday gift by my side. He let me choose between a new radio and his old battered one with short-wave capabilities. He knew me so well.

Listening to Hawaiian stations, and eligible for discounts through my job in the World Travel Department, plans to visit Hawaii materialized.

Other plans materialized as well.

Exploring each other in the dark and mystic nights on beaches meant nothing to the U.S. Navy. The *Mahan* reported to the Long Beach shipyards for maintenance and repairs, forcing us into a new schedule. Dave began taking a Greyhound bus from Long Beach to San Diego, still stopping at the Locker Club and calling me to pick him up.

Enter Donnie Casey. Stationed on the *Mahan* with Dave, the two became good friends, and after Donnie bought a red Triumph TR-3 roadster, they often drove to San Diego.

Soon deciding to visit their families, they headed for Dallas and Donnie's parents. From there, Dave boarded a bus for Dublin, Georgia, and visited his parents and younger sister for a few days.

Dave and Donnie may have made it as far as the Arizona state line before the lid blew off the simmering pot we called our apartment.

Sande knew the Marine from Twentynine Palms planned to visit that weekend, but when he arrived, she was nowhere to be found. We entertained him while she entertained her boss.

I hate confrontations, but this breached even my limits. Alice and I marched into her bedroom Monday morning, lump in my throat and sweaty palms aside, and I walked to her bedside.

"Listen, not doing your share of the cleaning around here is one thing, but what happened this weekend was something else. You knew he was coming here, and you left us to deal with him. The poor guy didn't know what to do or say to us."

Sitting up, back against her wooden headboard, she stared at me, then Alice, then back at me.

No reaction.

"We're done. You need to find your own place, and get out of here." She was in her own nearby apartment within the week.

I learned from Bob that Dave, quietly observing the mess we called home, planned to evict Sande if I did not. He is the only man, other than my father, who ever wanted to protect me from the vagaries of life.

***

With Dave's return from Texas and Georgia, my introduction to human anatomy resumed.

We played at sex. I still refused to say "yes," but he was allowed to go where no man had gone before. Clothing created temporary barriers easily conquered.

One barrier came down on a Sunday morning after I picked him up at my parent's house, and we made our way to an empty apartment.

"Where are Alice and Bob?" he asked as I unlocked the front door.

"They planned to go out to eat after church this morning."

"You mean we have the place to ourselves?" A rhetorical question as he led me to our sofa.

"For a while."

"Sounds good to me."

"Me too."

Sprawling out the length of the sofa, we faced each other, his left arm cradling my head. Kissing him, I leaned back looking into those hazel eyes, then closed mine and kissed him again.

Now comfortable feeling him through corduroy, my left hand slid down in front of him. I felt every inch of him as my hand traveled down his jeans until he wrapped his hand around my wrist, gently moving it back up to his hip. Within seconds, he guided my hand down, folding my fingers around him.

Feeling his curve, his taunt warm flesh, I stayed for a moment, unsure of what to do. Then I released him.

I felt his soft kiss on my forehead.

THAT SUMMER

After roommate problems, long road trips and living with the *Mahan* over a hundred miles away, we needed a day to soothe jangled nerves. Ocean waves beckoned.

On Saturday, June 27, we piled into Bob's car and headed for Silver Strand State Beach south of San Diego.

The cool, ground-hugging fog parted as Bob crept through the parking lot. With few beach goers there before us, we picked out a fire ring close to the pavement, and wrestled picnic supplies from nooks and crannies of the trunk.

Arms loaded and trudging through deep sand, we faced a strong onshore breeze as we headed for our chosen spot. Bob manhandled the ice chest, Dave lugged a cardboard box filled with splintered pieces of wood, and Alice and I brought up the rear with food, clothes hangers and my tattered white chenille bedspread.

"Ouch! Damn it!"

Hearing Alice utter a rare swear word, I turned in time to see her drop straight down on the sand and rip off her tennis shoes without untying them. She got back up carrying the offending culprits along with everything else.

Jagged sand crystals grinding into tennis shoes had the rest of us limping by the time we reached the fire ring. Dumping our cargo, shoes were pulled off with sighs of relief after lose sand squeezed between red, irritated toes.

Unfurling my old bedspread, Dave and Bob pinned down two

sides down with firewood and the ice chest, while Alice and I used bags of food to prevent the remaining sides from becoming airborne. Anchors in place, we sat down in a semi-circle around the fire ring. Not for long.

"My butt doesn't match what I'm sitting on," Alice moaned, shifting her weight in multiple directions at the same time.

"You're not the only one." Hearing Bob complain, we knew we were in trouble.

Crawling on hands and knees, butts bumping into butts, we shoved sand back and forth through chenille. Laughing until we hurt, we resigned ourselves to the lumps and bumps of life on the beach.

Settled down again, and facing a royal blue Pacific, the tide's rhythmic sloshing and salty sea breeze soothed us...for two minutes.

Crunching dried twigs announced Dave was hungry. After he put handfuls in the center of the fire ring, Bob, matches clenched between teeth, arranged chunks of wood in a pyramid. Motioning Dave back, he shoved a burning match deep into his masterpiece.

Alice and I could no longer ignore the hints.

We started straightening clothes hangers, and after sufficient well-timed grunts and groans, the guys commandeered the job from us. Turning to the food, she and I set out marshmallows, hot dogs and the fixings on our improvised dining room table, and opened for business.

With few words, and stomachs no longer growling, we huddled over the remains of our fire, lazily dipping marshmallows into the embers. Distracted by Dave's arm around me, his hand on my left thigh, I needed his supervision.

Cinders never tasted so good.

Stomachs full, and the edge taken off raw nerves, we spent the afternoon rehashing our apartment escapade and the hassles caused by the *Mahan* moving to Long Beach. Alice and Bob must have been there; someone snapped pictures of Dave holding me close and laughing through the marshmallows I stuffed in his mouth.

The western sun dipping into the ocean said it was time to push sandy feet back into shoes and head home. The last shade of light faded as Bob and Alice walked to our front door, and Dave and I drove to my parent's house.

"Oh, I like that song." He reached over, turning up the volume on the radio to listen to 'Little Children' by Billy Kramer.

Him and kids.

Just as it ended, we rolled to a stop at my parent's front door.

Reaching out with both arms, he held me close, and we exchanged a slow, sweet kiss.

"I suppose we're a little too young yet to make plans to get married right now." I felt his eyes watching me through the darkness.

"Yeah, we probably are a little too young yet."

A quick kiss good night and he left.

We had forever to make those plans.

WHERE ARE YOU?

Bob, Alice and I each had three days off for the 4th of July holiday beginning Friday, July 3. Dave could not leave the ship until Saturday morning, but he did not miss anything. Unable to find spectacular fireworks, we opted for a quiet weekend at home both nights.

A relaxing Sunday evening put us in a mellow mood. Bob kicked off his shoes and settled down on our sofa, so Dave sank into the recliner across from him. I poured a round of cold drinks, and as Alice passed them out, I hit the TV's on button. Finished playing hostess, she curled up against Bob and I sat on the floor along Dave's right side.

With my left shoulder leaning against the recliner, his right hand fondled a curl of hair lounging over my eye, wrapping it around his finger. The high school class ring on his other hand sparkled, reflecting light from a nearby floor lamp.

But decisions needed to be made. The coming Friday, July 10, was Dave's 21st birthday.

"Okay, so what are the plans for your birthday?" I asked, twisting to face him.

"Right now, the plan is to start the party in Long Beach Friday night. Then Donnie and I will bring it to San Diego the next morning."

Oh, oh.

"Ah, you are going to hide the car keys aren't you?"

"Yeah, don't worry. We'll bring the party down here by bus

Saturday morning." He flashed his best Mona Lisa at me.

"Hey, look at the time. I need to get you down to the Locker Club."

He checked his imported Seiko wristwatch.

"No, it's okay. There's one last bus to Long Beach later tonight. I'll catch it."

At 10 p.m., with a damp coastal breeze whipping through open car windows, we drove through a warm summer's night. Arriving minutes later at the Locker Club, and knowing he was rushed for time, I parked alongside the building with the engine running.

Summer shorts and sticky leather upholstery brought a whimper when my bare legs pulled free to stretch across the front seat. Meeting me halfway, he gave a sympathetic "ouch," and laughed that laugh.

"You guys have fun Friday, and I'll see you Saturday." I watched hazel eyes darkened by shadows.

"We will. I'll call you from the bus station Saturday morning." A quick kiss and he hurried out the door to catch the all-important last bus to Long Beach.

He usually watched me drive off, but not this night. This night, July 5, I watched him rush into the Club.

Blue and white plaid shirt, light tan cords, white tennis shoes.

Old Spice rode home with me.

***

Dave celebrated his milestone birthday with friends in Long Beach Friday night, while the three of us watched TV in San Diego.

"Well, tomorrow's going to be a long day you guys. I'm going to try to get some sleep." Standing up, I stretched and headed toward my bedroom. "Good night."

"Yeah, I need to get back to the Base," Bob said, pushing himself up off the sofa.

"I guess I better get some sleep too," Alice chimed in, standing up to kiss Bob goodnight.

The next morning, Bob picked Alice up and they headed

for the local Mall, while I gulped down a glass of milk and got dressed. My car keys sat poised next to the telephone.

At noon, I camouflaged a slice of bologna with mustard and perched on a kitchen barstool near the phone to watch our unmoving wall clock.

The guys must have slept in after partying all night.

Alice and Bob, exhausted after picking out birthday gifts for family in Iowa, stumbled through our front door in the middle of the afternoon.

"Are Dave and Donnie here?" Alice asked, dumping her collection along the sofa.

"Nope, haven't heard a word from them. They probably partied late and slept in."

"Yeah, they'll get here soon," Bob called out, jogging toward our bathroom.

By 8:00 p.m., we were eating delivery pizza and watching a rerun of The Jackie Gleason Show.

Maybe tomorrow. Maybe he meant Sunday.

The phone did not ring Sunday.

Where is he?

It did not ring the next day.

Or the next.

Maybe he found someone else in Long Beach. He knows he doesn't owe me anything. No, Dave being Dave, he would tell me if that happened.

Maybe something happened to him. No, Donnie would call me.

No matter which answer I tested, nothing felt right.

I never discussed the possibilities with anyone. I knew everyone assumed he was a no-show because of another woman.

A week or so later, I mailed a letter to the *Mahan* telling him I wanted no explanation, but asking him to let me know he was okay. It went unanswered.

My letter hasn't come back, so he got it. He doesn't want to talk to me.

Questions still nagged at me. I began checking the ship movements listed in the San Diego newspaper every week.

The Mahan has the answer.

***

August and September showed up, and so did two distractions.

Bob paraded another eligible sailor through our apartment. Chuck seemed okay, but no bells rang, at least none of mine. He regularly asked me out however, and I regularly accepted, content to stay the course while plowing through ship movement lists.

My vacation in Hawaii did a better job of distracting me.

Maybe Dave got mad about me planning to go to Hawaii. No, that would not bother him.

It was mid-September when I landed on Oahu for two weeks of touring the four Big Islands. Surf, tropical breezes and available men.

Dave doesn't care. Why should I?

My first few days were spent visiting the usual tourist spots, and being fawned over by hotel and tour representatives. Then I flew to Kauai.

The part-time tour guide, full-time cop and I talked until 3:00 a.m. He invited me along on his tour the next day, and that evening, drove me to the airport for my flight back to Honolulu. Taxiing down the runway that night, with promises to write, I wondered why I was leaving.

There's nobody waiting for me at home. Damn it Dave, where are you?

JULY 10, 1964

The sole of Donnie's right shoe ripped back to its heel as he buried it in the brake pedal. It did not matter.

The TR-3 roadster scaled the cement barricade, diving headlong into a San Diego Freeway support pillar. Ricocheting off it, the vehicle somersaulted three times as it sailed over unsuspecting drivers going in the opposite direction. Landing upside down on Willow Street, it slid toward an oncoming car, but that did not matter either. Neither Dave nor Donnie were still in the roadster.

On Saturday morning, July 11, 1964, the Long Beach Independent newspaper described Dave and Donnie as being "smashed to death," and closed its front page story with "…Alligood was observing his 21st birthday Friday."

DAVE'S GONE

There it is! The Mahan's back.
On the morning of November 6, 1964, the days-old newspaper fluttered down across the table in the Auto Club's break room. I raced for my desk telephone.

"Hey Dad, the *Mahan*'s back in town. Would you please do me a favor, and call the ship? You don't need to talk to Dave, just ask if he's on board so I'll know he's okay."

At 6:00 p.m., my father lightly tapped on our apartment door. No hello. No formalities.

"Dave's gone. He was killed in a car wreck. Whoever answered the telephone on the ship said he was dead, and I just hung up. I had to call back to find out what happened."

Shaking his head, he looked down and turned away, slowly walking back to his car.

"No! God, no!"

The sofa stopped my fall when Alice dashed from behind me, running for our telephone.

"Bob, get over here! We just found out Dave was killed in a car wreck!"

Backing down onto our sofa, unable to see, I hugged myself to stop sobs hacking into my ribs.

"No, no!"

Alice's own tear-filled eyes met mine as she sat down next to me, her arm around my shoulders.

Still sobbing when Bob and Johnny arrived, they guided me

into the back seat of Bob's car.

What if he lived for a while after the accident? What if he lay somewhere dying?

Boarding the *Mahan*, Bob managed to get Deacon, a younger friend of Dave's, off the ship.

"I don't know how to tell you all this," he whispered, staring across the dashboard. He looked over his shoulder at me.

"I called a San Diego operator, I did. We tried to find you, but couldn't figure out how to spell your last name," he stammered, falling silent again.

I can't stand this.

"Please, Deacon. What happened?"

He needed a deep sigh before continuing.

"The night of his birthday, he had duty, so I told him I'd stand by for him. I'm too young to drink, and he and some of the guys wanted to hit a bar to celebrate."

A deeper sigh.

"The party started when he got off work at 4 o'clock, and according to the guys, around 6 o'clock, he decided he wanted to head for San Diego. He and Donnie drove to a friend's house in Long Beach to pick up some street clothes they kept there, and then they headed out of town."

His voice trembled, holding back unseen tears. We all knew he idolized Dave.

"I heard they...they made it as far as Willow Street in Long Beach. The cops thought an Oldsmobile might have clipped their fender, and flipped them into oncoming traffic. Anyway, they said both of them died at the scene, so the ship sent me down to identify Dave. I couldn't have done it if he hadn't been wearing his class ring. I guess they sent somebody else to identify Donnie."

Poor innocent Deacon, innocent no more.

His right hand reached across the back of his seat.

"Here are the addresses for their families in case you want them."

He pressed a damp, wrinkled note into my hand, and unable

to say goodbye, climbed out of the car and followed the pier lights back to the *Mahan*.

I stared at the nothingness outside my window.

"Can we just go home?"

***

Rolling into a tight ball that night did nothing. Dave was still dead, and I was still thankful for the unthinkable.

Thank God he died right away. He didn't lay there thinking about dying, wondering why I wasn't with him. Was he in pain? Did he know he was going to die?

Tossing and turning did not help.

Why do divorced people get so upset? They might see each other again in the grocery store or out on date night. Dave doesn't even exist now.

Long hours ticked away.

What if I hadn't been so stubborn about virginity? His feelings wouldn't have been the same. He would've stayed with his friends.

The first hint of daylight framing my window shades brought darker thoughts.

If he hadn't decided to see me, he'd still be alive. Why couldn't I have died instead of him? He was so young…he had so much to live for.

Rolling onto my stomach, I buried my face in a wet pillow, the first of many.

Unable to face the outside world, I telephoned two friends with the news on Saturday, and spent that day and Sunday hiding in our apartment.

In spite of my intentions, Monday arrived, and the dense cloud swirling around my head stayed with me. My friends at work knew what happened, and by 9:30 in the morning, so did everyone else.

I could not face them, but it did not matter. No one knew what to say to me anyway. Walking into our file room and break room brought an uncomfortable quiet, then nervous chatter until I walked out.

My gruff, no-nonsense boss passed behind my desk chair, gently patting me on the head.

A co-worker remembered being stuck in traffic after a horrendous accident on Willow Street in Long Beach last July.

Taking dictation, filing and answering phones kept me focused during the days, but then there were the nights.

Stumbling out of my bedroom late one evening, hunting for solace in hot chocolate, Bob whispered to Alice, "I wish she'd just scream."

I wish I had.

Please, please let the next 30 years go by fast. It won't hurt so bad by then.

I told myself over and over that life had to not only go on, but go on with "a stiff upper lip." I had to get through this.

The eye doctor did not care when I answered questions in a yes or no fashion, and I made it out with the girls on Friday nights, silent tears often dancing with me.

Saturday nights came along regularly, and so did Chuck. Bob told him about Dave, but he never said a word, acting as if nothing happened. However, when he developed a roll of film for me, he had Bob deliver the prints. It contained two pictures of Dave at our beach fire ring the day we talked about getting married.

My friends never left me alone for the next six months. If I was home by myself, Bob or Johnny stopped in to visit. Bob took me to Mass with him a few times, putting me in a place where I could still the voices in my head. It was a refuge without answers.

Bob's discharge from the Navy loomed in the near future, so Alice moved back to Iowa to wait for his return, and I moved back into my parent's house. I told myself it was because I could not afford to keep our apartment.

My parents never knew how Dave's death affected me, and I never told them or anyone else, how Dave and I talked about marriage a few days before he died. Everyone only knew I wired flowers to his grave on his birthday and at Christmas, so he became "that nice boy Carol dated who was killed in a car wreck."

Then something else happened that I did not discuss with anyone.

On my drive home from work shortly after moving back in with my parents, a strange sensation overwhelmed me.

Driving east on Interstate 8 and crossing over Mission Gorge Road, I knew a horrible accident was about to happen. The lead story on the evening news that night covered a woman being decapitated when her vehicle plunged off Interstate 8 onto Mission Gorge Road.

It was not the first time something like that crept into my head. The first happened in early 1963, while doing breakfast dishes one morning. A sudden overwhelming sense of sadness hovered over me, not depression, but a feeling of something bad about to happen. A few weeks later, Dave and I met.

Coincidences? Wild guesses? Did I deliberately forget both?

Slowly, my intense pain eased as I learned coping skills. Had I turned to alcohol or drugs, perhaps I could have worked through my grief, and then left those remedies behind. No, I needed something more complex, something to last a lifetime.

HE CAN'T BE HERE

Consciously or subconsciously, Chuck took advantage of my vulnerability by forcing me into a corner over marriage. When I could no longer stand his touch, I said I needed time apart, but a master of making me feel sorry for him, I ended up back with him time and time again.

By the summer of 1965, I could not resist traveling at cut rates or the opportunity to get away. I scheduled flights to Paris, and then on to London to join a tour group, with my itinerary including time in Dallas, Texas, and Dublin, Georgia.

Donnie's parents handled their tragedy by keeping his bedroom exactly as he left it; bed neatly made and everything in its proper place. It was a tribute to their only child.

Reaching into the clothes-filled closet, his father held out Donnie's right shoe. Its sole had been ripped back to the heel in his frantic, last ditch effort to stop the flight of the roadster. His mother stood in the doorway, red-stained eyes slowly moving across his room from left to right.

Was it difficult for them to meet me? I wish I had told them I never blamed Donnie, but how do you put something like that into words?

Their son drove the vehicle that night, and the police believed alcohol may have been involved. I knew he took his role as designated driver seriously, but after all, it was his friend's special birthday celebration. Maybe Donnie did have a drink or two, or maybe they were just having fun and not paying attention to the road. It no longer mattered. One careless moment ended their lives.

Traveling on to Dublin, I walked into a living room surrounding a huge color version of Dave's professional photograph. All other traces of him were gone...except for his grave.

I needed to visit his grave. It was the only place I could ever be with him again.

Sitting down with his family over a dinner of boiled okra and pickled peaches, we made the usual small talk. Georgia weather compared to California, busy airports, where I planned to visit in Europe.

"Do you want to drive over to the cemetery?" His mother sounded unsure.

"Yes. Yes, I'd like to."

More small talk all the way to the cemetery. Maybe talking about his death made it real. When she stopped along the side of the hardtop road, I knew it was real.

Sliding out of my seat, I closed the door behind me and watched her cross over to my side, then walk straight out. The freshly mowed grass smelled sweet, the warm sun comforting.

Following behind her, she abruptly stopped at the edge of a simple flat headstone resting in a grassy pillow.

James David Alligood
July 10, 1943 - July 10, 1964

I stared into the earth hiding his body. I was on his left side, exactly where I would have been in life.

This can't be all that's left of him. A body in the ground under a stone marking his death on his 21st birthday. He can't be here, not really. But if not here, where?

The grass and sun no longer soothed me.

Does she blame me? Why shouldn't she? He was coming to me and it got him killed. I wish I was alone so I could talk to him.

I did not know what to say on our way home. What could I

possibly say to make it easier for her? "I'm sorry your only son died because of me?"

His sister and I stayed in touch for a few years, and could have been great friends. During a second visit I made with my parents months later, she commented, "I would have liked having you for a sister-in-law." I found myself wondering how much he told his family about us.

And so a day after that first visit to Dublin, I got on with life by sightseeing in Western Europe, and returning to continued separations from Chuck.

Then during one such separation, a mutual friend made his move.

Cliff Martindale always knew when I free lanced it from Chuck. Not only were the two friends, but I had even introduced Cliff to a girlfriend of mine. For the first time, they were not together at the same time Chuck and I were taking a time out.

A cute, sweet guy, Cliff picked me up at 3:00 a.m. one morning for a day of fishing at a local lake.

DEJA VUE

Other than Cliff's concern for his mother's health, he was unimpressive, and I suspect I would have lost interest in him had the Navy not issued drastic orders. He would join the Marines stationed at a fuel depot in Chu Lai, South Vietnam.

He dropped off the face of the earth.

No phone call, no anything.

Please, not again...

He was "not here" when I called the neighborhood lounge we frequented, so in a frantic effort to find him, I kept calling friends. One eventually confessed he was at the lounge and staying in a drunken stupor.

What I did next would land me in jail today. I became a night stalker.

Wanting back-up while parked outside a bar in the middle of the night, I invited Sande along as a co-conspirator. Having stayed friends through all our problems, she agreed to sit with me into the wee hours of the morning.

On our very first night of surveillance, we watched him stagger out of the bar, wobble to his car and open the driver's side door.

Throwing my car door open, I jumped out and ran across the street. Having navigation problems sliding onto his front seat, he never saw me coming.

I jerked the outside door handle so hard he lost his grip on the inside handle. Shocked by the sudden absence of his door, he sobered up enough to realize I was in his face.

"Listen, if you don't want to see me, fine, but tell me so," I said in my best monotone voice. "I can't stand not knowing what's going on."

His right hand jerked forward, stabbing his key in the general direction of the ignition. Unable to steady his aim, he slumped back in his seat, staring out the windshield.

On eye level with him, my face inches from his now bowed head, I watched him wipe tears away.

"I can't do it," he mumbled. "I can't go to Vietnam knowing you're waiting for me. I'm not coming back. I can feel it. It's better if we don't see each other again."

"I don't believe that. You'll come back. You'll be okay, and you'll come back. I know you will."

He didn't mean to hurt me—he's afraid of dying!

Lifting his head, he stared straight in front of him.

"Are you sure, really sure? Do you still want to keep seeing me?" He rubbed his eyes with the back of his hand.

"Yes, I'm sure," came out of me in a now trembling voice.

Three weeks later, the Navy flew him to Vietnam, and five weeks after that, my 'Dear Joan' letter arrived. He was going to die. Do not wait for him.

Why was he so afraid of Vietnam? Only once did he talk about his time with a patrol unit in the early 1960s. It worked inside Laos, our secret war, in maneuvers later revealed to be the Barrel Roll Operation. Its mission was to rescue two downed pilots, which it did successfully. However, the pilots received heavy ground fire as they descended by parachute, the terror of which caused one to lose his grip on reality by the time he landed.

And so, heartbroken, I bogged myself down with evening classes, friends and casual dates. I would keep busy until he returned.

***

With all my gal pals married or on the verge of marriage, I

looked for replacements and found them in three older, let us say more worldly women. Each bent on landing all four of us in jail, I safely graduated with a degree in Life on the Wild Side in early October of 1967, mere days before answering 'the' telephone call.

"Hello."

"Hi, Carol."

"Cliff?"

"Yeah."

"When did you get back?"

"A few weeks ago."

"And you're just now calling me?"

"I didn't know what to say, so when I got back, I took leave, and went to see my folks."

He sounds so sweet.

"I told Mom about you. How you're the kind of girl a guy marries. Can we talk?"

"Yeah, I guess so."

It's so good to hear him.

He knocked on the front door an hour later.

"Want to get a hamburger? We can go up to the Mall or on into San Diego if you want."

"The Mall's fine."

He looks so lost.

After we got into his El Camino, he did not move. My appetite was long gone anyway.

"Listen, I know I really messed up. I didn't mean to hurt you, and I never stopped loving you. I thought about you all the time while I was over there. Is there any way we can work this out?"

"I don't know." I looked down at the limp hands in my lap, realizing they were mine.

Do I love you?

"Please think about it. I love you. I need you." He choked up, pressing his forehead into crossed arms hugging his steering wheel.

Need. Need?

"We can get married whenever you want to. It's up to you."

He finally looked directly at me, tears welling up in frightened brown eyes.

He's so scared.

I wanted to wrap him in love and protect him from the world.

Our Christmas-themed wedding, set for December 22, 1967, would happen in San Diego's famed Balboa Park.

IS THIS ALL THERE IS?

Sculpted hedges, towering trees, even Cabrillo Bridge over Highway 365, were decked out in splashes of color. Red, white and green lights plunged off ornate Spanish Baroque buildings left over from the 1914 Panama-California Exposition. Twinkling archways spanned sidewalks, luring visitors from one tourist attraction to another. One was St. Francis Chapel.

The gold-gilded Spanish altar from the 1600s over whelmed you when you first entered the chapel. Only after absorbing it, did you notice the sparse brown ceramic floor and rough wooden pews. The rustic chapel engulfed visitors in early California history.

**

My street-length white wedding dress, red roses and short veil, along with Sande's matron of honor green velvet dress, completed our Christmas wedding. Well, our 'almost' Christmas wedding. It did fall short of the holiday, just as it would fall short of a real marriage.

We exchanged our vows in St. Francis Chapel before immediate family, splitting the cost of our gold bands between us. After Sande's husband posed us for a round of pictures, it was off to my parent's home for a reception in their decorated garage.

Unable to afford a honeymoon, we spent our first night as husband and wife in a newly rented apartment. There, my once-in-a-lifetime night laid the tracks for the train wreck coming down the rails.

Yes, I was still a virgin. Yes, I expected a man who was two years older than me, spent time in foreign ports, and fathered two children in a previous marriage, to be an experienced lover.

After satisfying himself four times, I laid there.

The rest of our sex life could have been done by remote control. It became a version of "slam, bam, thank you ma'am," almost every night of every week. He told me surgery could cure my problem.

At least his job in the engine room on the *USS Hanson*, a ship moored in San Diego Harbor, meant he came home after work every night. Well, except the night deja vu struck again.

No Cliff coming through the door after work.

No phone call.

He's gone again! Did something happen to him? Was there an accident in the engine room?

He found me sprawled across our bed crying because of a simple miscommunication.

Next, we paid our first visit to his parents in Phoenix. Preoccupied with my mother-in-law's rants about how he could have "made it" with two of his former girlfriends, I missed the calligraphy sprawled across her bedroom wall.

I should have paid attention when my father-in-law served her coffee in bed. Then he and I washed dishes while Cliff and his younger brother lay across the bed with her, reading the Sunday newspaper.

Three months later, the Navy did it again. The *Hanson* shipped out to Viet Nam, taking Cliff with it. Service men were not supposed to return to Vietnam for six months, but at least he felt safer on a ship.

However, when he was due for re-enlistment while at sea, all he wanted from the Navy was out. A few months shy of ten years of service, he flew home from Da Nang, South Vietnam, much to the chagrin of his mother.

"He'll never make it on the outside," she predicted. I knew better. He had me.

***

After settling into married life with my well-paid secretarial job in Chula Vista, and Cliff's job as a driver for Goodwill in San Diego, perception became my reality.

I believed I was the bread winner, second mother, sex toy, house slave and sole care taker of Misty, a silver toy poodle. We introduced her to my parents as their granddaughter.

Near the end of our third year together, I had my bathroom revelation. I always did my best thinking there.

It started one morning with the secretary for the director over my two bosses. I was in no mood for the Queen Bee's attitude after a run-in with one of my bosses who had a 'hands' problem. I tolerated him because we needed the good money I earned, especially after Cliff walked off his own job.

Walking through her door in my new navy blue suit, she glared at my knees.

"Carol, that skirt just isn't you."

It's not even a mini skirt!

"Really? I bought it last weekend because I liked the way it looks."

Handing over my paperwork, I walked out and straight into the ladies' room. Slamming a stall door behind me, a revelation slammed back.

Is this all there is?

ON THE ROCKS

How I felt about our marriage, real or perceived, was irrelevant.

I remained a virgin until my wedding night because that was how I was raised. Now my goal was to never get a divorce, especially for something as trivial as no longer loving my husband. Not complaining however, meant no one knew how frustrated I was, nor how consigned to making this marriage work.

Who was I to complain anyway? In our years together, Cliff never raised a hand to me, did not even act like he wanted to get physical. He never stepped outside our marriage vows, or stayed out all night with friends.

We merely existed.

If we could not buy entertainment, we did not know what to do with our time. When I questioned how to pay for a collector's rifle, another car, or the tab for dinner with friends, I heard "You'll figure out a way. You always do."

Sex continued in pure boredom. Well, other than when we thought I might be pregnant after going off birth control pills for health reasons. It became very exciting, very fast.

Considering my bread winner status, child support payments for his two girls in Washington State and his lack of interest in those girls, I panicked. I held tight to the recent passage of Roe v. Wade, but he was not of the same mindset.

Ecstasy set in when my fears proved unfounded, and the incident frightened him into a vasectomy.

After he found another stable job, we purchased a home in a rural canyon east of San Diego, and 'went country.' Two beautiful collie brothers, Blue and Cheyenne, joined Misty, as did a neighbor's abandoned cat, Twerp, and Morrissa, a stray cat. So began our menagerie.

Cliff's friend from work, along with his wife, routinely trotted through our neighborhood on horseback, and it was more than Cliff could bear.

The friend helped us with horsemanship when we bought Cliff's horse, Baron, a mountain of an animal with a disposition making ownership of a horse one of the easiest things we ever did. The next step was finding a horse for me.

First was a beautiful, emotionally broken horse Cliff purchased from our former landlord sight unseen. She tried to kill anyone on her by taking them over backward, putting her in the same category as the retread tires Cliff consistently put on the front end of my car.

I cannot blame him for Cherokee however, but then I can blame him for the financial fiasco involved. After the horse ran away with me, our next door neighbor bought it with the promise of payment. The money never arrived, and Cliff refused to ask for it.

Feeling guilty, the neighbor's wife gave me a handmade turquoise, shell, and coral necklace in exchange for her husband's neglect. I had no idea how he felt about her bending his silver hashish spoon into a pendent.

This was where Danny Boy came into my life, and we did have some good times riding with Cliff and Baron. They would not last long.

We now had a family of critters, and decided it was time to move again.

Still within San Diego County, we landed in what locals call the East County. Living there was a point of pride for those willing to battle raging Santa Ana winds strong enough to topple semi-trucks, wild fires, rattle snakes, mountain lions, bobcats, packs of coyotes, illegal immigrants walking through your property, and trekking over 4,000 ft. Laguna Pass in snow. Wimps not allowed.

Our first stronghold was a rented mobile home near Campo, and new neighbors Del and Old Joe.

Del became a good friend, while Old Joe became the subject of my intuition again. Passing him one afternoon, *he's a dead man* flashed through my head. Two days later, he was found beaten to death for his Social Security check. My third premonition, like the previous two, was ignored.

Within months, we purchased a small house on five acres less than a mile from the Mexican border. Having little of our own money, we borrowed from my parents and floated a small second mortgage from good neighbor Del, in order to get into the property.

Sitting alone on a hill topped with dozens of pine trees, our driveway connected to a one-lane private dirt road. We had no telephone, no immediate neighbors, and overlooked a broad valley below whose farthest reaches included Mexico.

I loved it.

Cliff worked for a commercial egg-laying company in Campo, and they eventually offered him a managerial position. He turned it down; too much responsibility. Meanwhile, I drove 55 miles one-way into San Diego every day to an office job at the University of San Diego Hospital.

Then the beginning of the end manifested one sunny Saturday morning.

"It's good exercise," I mused aloud from Danny's corral.

"Yeah, it really is," Cliff chimed in from his work in Baron's corral.

Dragging my rake lifted a wisp of dust into the dry Southern California air. As it settled down over pods of manure prickled with tufts of alfalfa, Cliff lifted his own rake over the top metal rung of Baron's corral. Dropping it to the ground, he wedged himself between the lower rails, retrieved the rake and walked to our storage shed.

"Hey, I need to go use the head. Can you finish up okay?" he asked.

"Yeah, bring me a shovel."

Carrying one to Danny's corral, he propped it up in the corner nearest me.

"Here. I'll see you inside."

"Okay. I'll come in as soon as I'm done here."

Spinning around, he headed for the house. That was the last time he carried a shovel. Oh, he continued making sure food went into the horses, but I became solely responsible for what came out of them.

Good exercise indeed.

Bored with Baron a few weeks later, Cliff traded him for two white-face heifers destined for the butcher shop. I worked hard to convince him at least one of the pure-bred animals should be saved for breeding.

We next ventured into business with a co-worker of his and their boss. We raised hogs on our place, the other employee raised goats—other than the two I made into pets—and their boss chipped in money and management skills. It sounded good.

Meanwhile, with Cliff continuing to spend beyond our means, I devised a wake-up call. I resigned from my job at University Hospital, hoping he would become more concerned about finances.

Another idea gone terribly wrong.

We ended up with less money available when it came time to pay bills. He did come up with an inventive solution however, since his ex-wife and her husband owned nine race horses. With us in financial never, never land, an attorney sent her a letter advising we could no longer send child support payments.

OVER THE CLIFF...ER...EDGE

I made difficult choices every week. Should I spend an evening at the bowling alley with Cliff and his league, or take a class on that same night? If I expressed interest in taking a class on a night when he was home—or in taking a shower alone—or explained why I did not believe in calling him at work every day—he told me I did not love him.

Then, with the beginning of the end already in sight, his mother rolled the final scene into our home with her luggage.

Coming to visit one weekend while I was in San Diego meeting a friend from out of town, she brought news about Cliff's ex-wife. She left her second husband in Washington State, and moved to the Los Angeles area with her two daughters.

By the time I arrived at home that afternoon, his two girls were scheduled to be bused to us for a visit, compliments of his mother.

How could he make a decision like that without talking it over with me? He doesn't so much as send them birthday cards, and now he doesn't even want to send child support payments.

All I could muster was "What am I, a piece of furniture in my own house?"

Visit they did, the very next weekend. At 12 and 13 years old, they had all the attendant problems one might expect in girls that age, and then some.

Cliff became so distraught wanting to play daddy after they left, I told him to go to Los Angeles and stay until he got it out of his system.

Before his truck kicked up dust at the end of our driveway Saturday morning, my wedding band landed in my jewelry box.

This is my second chance.

Driving to the lone telephone booth in town, I closed myself in it, and studied Red Mountain through smudged glass. Looming like the giant it was, it sheltered the valley below. Now I needed sheltering.

How will I take care of everything without a job? And what are my folks going to think about me getting a divorce? I'll only be the second one in my generation, and the family doesn't even count the first one.

I dialed my parent's telephone number, each digit a deliberate effort. Each dropped coin clanged louder than the last.

"Hello," my father answered.

"Hi, it's just The Kid."

"Hey, how's it going out there?"

"I need to talk to you guys. I might be asking for some help."

"Oh, oh. What's wrong?"

"Well, Cliff is off to LA to be a daddy, and I'm off to file for divorce."

I stopped breathing.

"We were wondering how long it was going to take you."

***

At the beginning of my first week of freedom, I drove to the San Diego County Courthouse and filed a 'do it yourself' divorce. Our business partner agreed to serve the papers on Cliff whenever he returned, so those wheels were set in motion.

Two days later, I checked out the community college in El Centro. After making the drive there and deciding it was too far away, I weighed my college options around San Diego while driving home.

Plans circulated through my head until I turned down my driveway. I stood on the brake pedal.

Oh, hell! Are those truck tire tracks?

First, the brown tailgate, then the rest of the truck. They led to a dejected Cliff blending in with the front door stoop.

Shit!

Parking alongside his truck, I got out and walked around its back bumper, steeling myself for a dreaded confrontation. Once again, I needed to kick someone out of their home.

"Why are you back so soon?"

"I can't take it. The kids scream all the time, and all we do is fight. I just can't do it," he whined.

"So come home to Carol?"

"Yeah, I wanna come home," he whimpered, without looking up.

Is he trying to look that small?

"I dropped the girls off at school this morning, and headed straight here." He sighed, raising his head.

"You did what?"

"I left them at school and drove here."

There's that damn puppy dog look.

"Did you explain anything to them?"

"I left them a note."

"You left them a note!"

"Yeah, I left them a note."

"Good lord! Go call them. Tell them it was a mistake, and that you'll see them soon."

"But what about us?"

I had no idea it would be this hard. He told me I did not love him any more until I agreed. Now only pity remained, but that did not make it easier.

"Listen, if you want to stay in San Diego, fine. We can still see each other, but in the meantime, I've filed for divorce. Go sign the papers and call the girls."

"Okay," a dejected sigh, followed by "but can I spend the night?"

"I suppose so."

I expected sex to be more imaginative that night.

How many times can I be wrong?

In the morning, we worked through the most important details of our impending split. Since we owed money to my parents and to Del for the second mortgage, Cliff offered to walk out of the property, leaving it to me. Chivalrous to a fault.

The second issue swept us toward World War III.

"By the way, I'd like to take Blue to LA with me. I think the girls would love having a dog."

I felt 'stark terror' etching itself across my forehead.

Good Lord, he doesn't even notice when they're sick. Blue'll end up running the streets of Los Angeles.

"Ah…I'm sure they would, but won't it be hard on the boys to split them up? I mean he and Cheyenne have been together since the day they were born."

I hoped his thoughtful expression meant wheels spinning in the right direction.

"I don't know." Still looking thoughtful, he gazed past me.

"And what about their age? Do you really want to split them up at their age?"

"Naw, I guess not. It's probably best if they stay together, and we sure don't have room for both of them up there."

Both of them? That'd land you in a damn court.

He spit out his memorable parting words as he sat on the end of our bed, jingling truck keys.

"You know, you've never needed anyone."

I regretted not thinking fast enough to say what I needed was a man.

I soothed my angst, in a fashion, months later. Since we married on December 22, 1967, our 10th wedding anniversary was in the cross hairs. On December 21, 1977, I hand carried our divorce papers through the Courthouse so we were officially divorced one day before our 10th anniversary. Somehow it made me feel better. Of course, I paid for the divorce.

There were no tears when Cliff disappeared down the driveway that morning, although friends said they would flow once the dust settled. The dust never rose. Tears fell when I sold

Danny because I could not afford to feed him.

I stumbled around in a fog for a few days as ten years of my life evaporated, but I still noticed the partially blind dog running along the freeway. I traded Cliff in for her. Gypsy's upkeep was cheaper, her tail wagged when she saw me, and when she whined, it was for a legitimate reason.

Did I save Cliff from a world that frightened him? If I did, it did not do him any favors.

***

Working part time for a temp agency kept me financially solvent for two and a half days, so I cobbled together a work schedule with three different employers. If I was at the auto parts house owned by the family who traded cattle for Baron, it was Monday, Wednesday or Friday. If I found myself once again taking a lunch break at University Hospital, it was Tuesday or Thursday. If I worked without a lunch break, it was Sunday, and I was in the local real estate office.

But how I loved single life on my mountain top!

After working 10-to-12 hour days, in my spare time—better known as the black of night—I fed and watered livestock, along with four dogs and two cats, and killed the three rattlesnakes threatening them. Aside from the work they created, my four-legged family provided constant companionship and comic relief.

Goats Miss B and Spiffy bounced me between amusement and cussing every day, and many late nights, they met me on the driveway as I arrived home from work. Happy once in their pen eating grain, I repaired fencing by the light of the moon, fixed a light dinner and showered before sitting down in front of my window on the world.

The cool, dry breeze coming up the ravine every evening carried the scent of pine from my trees. I studied Red Mountain's bell-shaped silhouette while its glowing sandstone gave way to grays, then black. The pool of lights twinkling in the valley below were divided in half by Buckman Springs Road, winding its way south to Campo, and disappearing before touching the

Mexican border.

I found peace in those hours spent staring into the valley's heart.

And so life was good on my mountain until one day, it was not. Realizing I would vegetate if I spent my entire life in front of a window with a view, I began considering a move out of state.

Then a visitor cinched the deal.

Long before the dogs barked, I heard the roar of a motorcycle. Walking out my front door, I watched Del crest my driveway, then coast to a quiet stop at my front gate. Pulling his helmet off, he hung it from a handlebar and straddled his Harley.

"Hi, Carol."

"Hi, Del. You out cruising in this beautiful weather?"

"Yeah, and I thought I'd stop by and talk to you about an idea I've got."

"Sure, what's up?" Moving closer to the gate, I rested my hands on top of the cross-piece board, but made no move to open it or ask him inside.

"You know I think a lot of both you and Cliff, and I'm sorry you two broke up."

"Yeah, thanks. It was a bad deal all the way around, but it worked out for the best."

What is he leading up to?

"Listen, it occurred to me that we could help each other out. How about if you move in with me? You could work part-time and go to school too."

I swallowed—hard.

I can't crawl into bed next to him.

"Thanks, but I don't think so Del. I'm actually thinking about leaving California all together."

"Gee, I'd hate to see you do that. You know I always liked the way you treated Cliff."

He liked the way I treated Cliff? There's a frying pan and a fire somewhere in there.

"Thanks for the offer, but I don't want to move in, and then right back out again. It wouldn't be fair."

"Okay, but think about it. If you decide to stay in California, and think it might work, let me know."

"I will, and thanks." I walked inside as he kicked started his motorcycle and headed back out my driveway.

As nice as he was, the offer was not worth the price. Besides, he was well off and sure of himself. No 'rescue me' sign blowing in that wind.

Soon after a telephone line reached my property, two things happened. I listed the house with a realtor, and I received a call from Del's ex-wife.

"I don't know if you saw the news Carol, but Del was killed in Tecate, Mexico."

"What!"

"He and his girlfriend went down there for the first ever running of the bulls. He didn't plan to enter it, but was walking the route when they let the bulls out early."

"I remember hearing on the news that somebody got killed, but I had no idea it was him."

"They don't think any of the bulls got him. It looked like he hit his head when he tried to climb over the fence to get out of the way, and fell backward. He even sat at a picnic table talking with everybody while he waited for the medics to check him out."

"I'm so sorry."

"Me too, but there's another reason why I needed to talk with you. Don't worry about paying off that second mortgage right away. Wait until everything goes through probate. Del added an amendment to his will that if something happened to him, your debt to him was to be considered paid off free and clear."

"You're kidding."

"No, so don't do anything. Just wait until everything is done."

After weeks of gossip about his girlfriend needing that money, one of his sons found an error in the will. The amendment was declared null and void.

It was time to leave. After all, there was a Native American man in Arkansas teetering on the brink of self-destruction.

IF IT'S TOO GOOD TO BE TRUE

California and I parted company in March of 1982. I left behind an unworkable marriage, and the graves of friends Misty, Morrissa and Twerp.

"Okay, the trailer's hooked up. I'm ready," I called out, looking over my shoulder at my father.

"Good, me too." Nodding toward the family friend standing next to me, he added "He can ride with you to spell you when you get tired of driving, and I'll take the lead."

My father pulled out towing a trailer carrying household goods, and with Cheyenne, Blue and Gypsy settled on the back floor of his car. Towing a second trailer stacked with more household items and our family friend, I slipped in behind him.

I drove the entire trip, and after one night in a questionable motel and a winding road into northwest Arkansas, we arrived at Lincoln. My recently purchased fixer upper, located 20 miles west of Fayetteville, stood on the outskirts of town.

After unloading our cargo, we checked into a motel for the night, and the next morning, deposited the trailers at a local U-Haul. As the two men left for California, I surveyed the projects ahead of me.

The older two-bedroom house, sitting on a large pie-shaped corner lot, needed TLC more than it needed major work. Its biggest selling point was the mobile home adjacent to the house; two homes for the price of one.

The previous owner's circular flower garden gracing the center of the front yard showcased her love for working outdoors. Too bad she did not work as much on the inside.

The house did lack my least favorite free loaders, roaches, but every floor-level kitchen cabinet housed mouse droppings 1/4" deep. They must have had names.

I spent my first full day on hands and knees wheedling vacuum attachments at eye level, scrubbing cabinet interiors, and setting mouse traps. I made a mental note to find a cat shelter.

Next, it was on to her storage unit, AKA garage.

Through the town newspaper, I found a young man who did odd jobs, including hauling trash. Showing up two days late, he first cleared a space on the garage floor to serve as his spittoon. After leaving with his final load for the local dump, I hosed out chewing tobacco.

Job hunting came next, and I soon landed a secretarial job in Siloam Springs about 20 miles from Lincoln. I was on my way.

Gaining state residency status a year later, I enrolled at the University of Arkansas campus in Fayetteville, and signed up for a smorgasbord of classes. Taste testing everything within reach, I also wrangled a part-time job right on campus.

However, although fading into memories, my drive to the Siloam Springs office did come back to haunt me like some outdated TV commercial. It was late night in the grungy, dilapidated Lincoln Laundromat.

Conscious of the well-built, broad shouldered man 20 feet from me, I gathered clothes from a dryer too far from the exit. Walking back and forth between the dryer and my folding table, his covert glances made me nervous.

"Don't you work up in Siloam Springs?" a sexy voice asked.

I stopped in mid stride, looking directly at him for the first time. The voice suited him well with his creased blue jeans, white cowboy hat and brilliant smile against a smooth Native American complexion.

"Yeah, I used to. How do you know?"

Looking out the Laundromat's only clean window, he nodded toward my car.

"I used to see that Ford of yours heading up Highway 59 every morning. My house is near the corner where you turned north to head up to Siloam Springs."

Oh, oh. How long has he been watching me?

My expression must have telegraphed my concern.

"Oh, don't worry, I'm not some stalker. I just started noticing the same car going by every day. I know where you live too. I see the car parked across from Posey's. Anyway, I'm Ray Mackey."

"Hi, I'm Carol, and yes, I used to work in Siloam Springs, and yes, I live across from the Poseys."

We engaged in more small talk before he broached what was on his mind.

"Listen, would you like to go to the Lincoln dance this Saturday? There'll be a good local band that does country western."

He's checked me for wedding rings.

"Thanks, but I don't date men I just met in a laundromat."

Do I sound nervous?

"Okay, I understand." He pulled a pencil and scrap of paper off the community bulletin board hanging alongside the front door.

"Do you know the Poseys across the road from you?"

"Sure."

"Okay, here's my phone number. If you're interested in going out, ask them anything you want about me. I've spent my whole life in this area, and I've even done some work for them. If they say I'm okay, and you're interested, give me a call and we'll go to that dance."

"Okay, I'll think about it."

Griping my clothes basket in front of me for a lethal weapon, I walked out into the dimly lit parking area. Ever so slightly turning my gaze, I made sure he stayed inside the building.

I called Mrs. Posey the next morning.

"Ray? Oh yeah honey, we've known him for nearly 30 years.

Folks around here use him like a veterinarian. In fact, we hired him a few years ago to do some artificial insemination on our cows when we wanted them bred to a top bull. The only thing is, honey, he's probably been married ten times."

That's a tall tale if I ever heard one. He's probably dated a lot.

I dialed Ray's number.

"Hello."

"Hi, it's Carol."

"So I guess you called Mrs. Posey. Did I pass inspection?"

"Yes, you did, and I'd love to go to the dance this weekend."

Half Cherokee, intelligent and good looking, he was a direct descendant of Sequoia who developed the tribe's written alphabet.

Working full time in a machine shop, he also provided artificial insemination and unlicensed veterinary care for local cattle growers, and was a former local rodeo rider. He still did weekend steer and calf roping with friends who considered him one of the last real cowboys.

A talented singer, guitar player, and excellent cook, he kept his house so clean it shamed most women. Loving kids and animals, he even climbed a spindly tree bordering the highway to rescue my newly adopted cat, Sabrina.

Remember the saying, the one starting with "if it looks too good to be true..."?

***

Several dates later, we headed into the back country for an evening jam session where Ray joined in with his guitar. The place rocked with traditional country music until a whiskey bottle guarding his right boot soured his chords. Putting his guitar under his arm, he staggered out the door.

What's this? I've never even seen him with a beer.

As I followed him, a too-made-up bleached blond followed me.

"Excuse me," she called out from behind me.

"Yes." I stopped moving, but kept a watchful eye on him.

"I was just wondering if you two are a couple."

"Ah...yes. Yes, we are."

"Okay, thanks. I wanted to ask before I talked to him." Disappointed, she turned back to the barn.

I should have asked her to send my common sense out to me, obviously having left it on a hay bale. Instead, I went into a fast walk to catch up with my drunken ride home.

Weaving a path toward the passenger side of his truck, Ray tossed the keys to me as I arrived at the truck's front bumper. Thankful he had no plans to drive, I pulled myself up behind the steering wheel, and drove us to an all-night restaurant, hoping he could walk inside.

Cliff, although drinking heavily before going to Vietnam, was not an alcoholic. My one grandfather was, but he never drank in front of me. Other than a friend of Cliff's who, decked out in black dress pants and crisp white dress shirt, urinated on himself, I had no idea how the disease worked.

Ray was a binge alcoholic. He stayed sober during the work week, but every other Saturday night, drank himself into oblivion. He always gave me the truck keys after his first shot, and I drove us to the same all-night restaurant. Then we went to his place, and I put him to bed.

Finding out he was an alcoholic, plus listening to his ravings about preferring blondes, would have sent the old naïve me out the nearest door with an exit sign swinging over it. This Carol suffered his comments about other women, so reminiscent of Rich in San Diego, along with his erratic temper.

I knew I could save him from his demon drink.

Hell knew Ray personally. Years before we met, his beautiful eldest daughter married a young man he did not like, so he stopped speaking to her. A month after her wedding, she and her husband were killed by a drunk driver in a head-on collision. A passerby who recognized her, called Ray, who then rode in the ambulance with her.

I do not know if he had time to tell her he loved her. He never talked about that night, other than saying she died in a car crash. He did brag about her horseback riding skills, and pointed out his wall-mounted photo display of her barrel racing in rodeos.

In his own version of reality however, he never condemned drunk drivers. He reserved condemnation for those driving while high on illegal drugs.

And so every second Saturday night, he held out his truck keys and I took them.

His daughter's death went a long way in explaining his alternate weekends. On those weekends, his only other child, a daughter 11 years old, came to visit.

On Friday nights, he gave me $20 with instructions to take her to Walmart to shop until his night shift ended.

The next night, she determined where we went, what time we left and what time we came home. Impressed with how he doted on her, it took time for me to understand she also controlled my life.

Unlike what I heard about many alcoholics, his temper surfaced when he was sober, never when he was drunk. I heard stories about sober Ray being so angry with a young calf, he swung a 2x4 at its head with such force he killed it with one blow. I heard about the fight with a man where he wielded a lug wrench as a weapon.

Drunk, he was mellow and loving.

Anger surged in him over the smallest things when sober, but I sensed when to shut up, so he never raised a hand to me. His friends assumed I put up with being beaten like his other women.

Afraid of physical pain, and worn out by the emotional ups and downs, I devised a plan to save this man I loved from the clutches of his illness. I had to hatch it at the right time, and that time came in early fall of 1984.

"Is your steak okay?" Cutting into his, he glanced at me.

"Great." I did not compliment him out of fear. The steak was perfect as usual.

He invited me for an early Sunday dinner because it was his last day of vacation before returning to work in the machine shop. Although still bothered by a fresh injury to his thumb from a calf-roping throw gone wrong, his upbeat mood continued.

Then his fork dropped to the floor between us, and by the time he picked it up, the entire world was out to get him.

A PRIVATE HELL

"I never had trouble with depression until about ten years ago, after my daughter died."
Retrieving the fork, he stared at it, turning it over and over in his good hand.

"That's why I sold my hand gun. I only keep a rifle around." He smoothed out the tablecloth before returning the errant fork to its place.

It was the first time he ever mentioned his state of mind, and I knew it was now or never. After he left for work the next morning, I made an appointment with his doctor for later that day.

***

"I know you can't discuss Ray's medical care with me, but I want to know if you're aware of his problems with depression."

The doctor did not look surprised.

"I've known for a long time that he's driven by something, but had no idea what. So what's going on with him?"

"Several years ago, his daughter was killed in a car wreck when he wasn't speaking to her, and I think it still haunts him. He's also bought into the stereotypes of lazy, fat Indians, so he's obsessed with watching his weight, keeping his house clean and working two jobs."

"Is it just depression, or are there other problems?"

"He's a binge alcoholic, but it's when he's sober that his temper gets the best of him."

"How bad does he get?"

"He's unpredictable and can be violent. He'll be fine one minute, and within seconds, if the least little thing goes wrong, the whole world is out to get him. He killed a calf with one blow from a 2x4, and used a lug wrench against a guy in a fight. There have been many times, if I hadn't shut up, I know he would have hit me."

Drumming his desk top, he looked at the floor between us, then at me.

"Okay, let's get him in here. I'll put him on a combination of medications and therapy. We need to get him started soon though, before he really hurts someone."

"Thank you so much. I'll figure out some way to get him here."

We shook hands, I opened the door and stepped toward the receptionist's desk.

My jaw dropped.

Ray's stare flew across the room, boring through me. In a few short steps, he stood next to me.

"What are you doing here?" he asked.

Fumbling for my checkbook killed enough time to wrap my head around what could happen.

He won't hurt me here, but what about later? What do I tell him...oh yeah, Mom and Dad are moving here next week.

"Oh, since my folks are retiring here, I decided to get them established with a doctor. You like this one so much, I thought I'd pay for a consultation to get them started with him."

Scribbling a barely legible check for the receptionist, she somehow managed to slip a receipt into my hand as I kept moving toward the exit.

I've got to get in my car.

"So why are you here?" I tried sounding nonchalant as we walked outside and crossed the parking lot.

Where are his hands?

"When I got to work, I checked in with the nurse to see what she thought about my thumb. It was a mistake. She wouldn't let me report for work without my doctor's release, so here I am."

"Well, that was probably a good thing. Listen, I need to get to the store to pick up some things, so I better go. I'll see you later. Bye."

I saw him watch my taillights until he could not possibly see them any longer.

At least I told him one truth. Needing a less expensive place in which to retire, my parents moved to Lincoln days later, and bought the property from me. I moved into the adjoining trailer and began paying rent.

***

"Hey, how about watching the big jackpot calf roping in Oklahoma this weekend? It'll be a while before I can rope again, but we could have breakfast somewhere and go watch them."

Huh? He's talking breakfast and jackpot roping like nothing happened.

The doctor started Ray on medications and they worked well, but he soon complained about taking so many pills and how they bothered his stomach. Suggesting he cut down on the dosage until his next appointment went nowhere. He decided if living meant taking all those pills, it was not worth it.

The pills ran out.

So did his good mood.

So did my safety net.

Where does he keep that rifle? Oh yeah, under his bed.

As much as I wanted to help him and would sacrifice almost anything, the one thing not on that list was my life. He would not be allowed to determine the expiration date on my tombstone.

I knew what had to be done, and knew if it was something his daughter wanted, he would agree to it. He would be furious with me later, and push me away for a time to punish me—that time was all I needed. More than anything, he had to believe it was his own idea.

When he mentioned his daughter's next weekend visit, I jumped on it.

"Hey, I said something to her about Hank Williams, Jr.,

coming to campus in a couple of weeks, and she acted like she'd really like to see him. Is it okay if I take her?"

"I suppose so," came his hesitant response. He never denied her anything, and as much as he detested colleges, I knew he would give his permission. He would keep himself in check until she had her night of fun, and deal with me later.

Hank, Jr. did not disappoint, and we actually had fun together that night. Then I slipped into an uneasy 'wait and see' mode.

He quietly seethed over my transgression, but was not sure how to unload his anger without involving his daughter. Then he invited me for another dinner.

We ate this one in silence, and while watching a Louis Gossett, Jr., movie on TV after dinner, took advantage of a commercial break to feed his horse.

A chunk of alfalfa sailed over the corral, landing squarely at the horse's front feet. I reached over the railing, patting the animal's sleek, muscular neck as it stretched for a mouthful of feed.

"That's a good movie," I said, "of course, Louis Gossett, Jr., is a good actor anyway."

"What? You one of those nigger lovers?"

He glared at me, stopping dead still for a few seconds before vaulting another stack of feed over the rail.

The anger smoldering beneath the surface found its vent and provided me with a reason to feign righteous indignation.

Now!

Giant steps marched me to the back screen door. Running inside, I snatched up my handbag, fishing my car keys out while stomping to the front door. After fumbling with the dead bolt, I jerked the door open, ran to my car and jumped behind the steering wheel. My shaking hand accidentally found the ignition.

Showering gravel as I jerked spinning tires out of his driveway, I chanced a quick look in my rear view mirror. His green and white GMC pickup crowded my back bumper.

Gunning my old Ford north toward the small town of Cincinnati, squealing tires slid sideways around the first curve.

Another furtive glance in the mirror revealed his truck swaying wildly as he negotiated the same curve.

Once on the straight-away, his pickup gained ground on me until we careened around a second curve. Coming out of it with more open road ahead, I floored the gas pedal through the straight stretch of road. Straddling the double yellow line, I crossed the old bridge in the river bottom before chancing another glance in my mirror.

He slowed down, then skidded off onto the shoulder in a cloud of dirt and gravel. His truck slipped from view as I rounded a third tree-filled curve.

Two days later, my father dropped me off at the Tulsa airport for an afternoon flight to Albuquerque, New Mexico.

Fascinated by mountains since age 10, they now meant wide open spaces, fresh mountain air and safety.

Ray would have to save himself.

WIDE OPEN SPACES

My first stop the next morning was the University of New Mexico (UNM) employment office.

After one completed job application, and a walk around campus, I hiked down famous Route 66 where it skirted the University. Wandering aimlessly under a brilliant blue sky, I found myself far down the road, approaching the New Mexico State Fair Grounds.

"Hey, need a ride?" a driver called out through his passenger window as he slowed to my pace.

"No thanks, I'm fine," I said, waving him off.

Giving me a disgusted look, he stepped on the gas and disappeared in traffic.

What a friendly town. That was the fifth guy to offer me a ride since I left the campus.

I learned more about that end of Central Avenue after I moved to Albuquerque.

Flying home the next day, I planned my escape.

He'll ignore me until after New Year's Day, so I'll have to leave before then.

Hang-up calls meant I was on his mind, so as soon as it warmed up enough after Christmas to not snow in the Texas Panhandle, I made my move.

With the trunk packed with clothes, the rest were piled on the back seat and floor of my car, weighed down by a 13" black and white TV and clogged steam iron. Stuffing a supply of cat food on the front passenger-side floor, I nested Sabrina in her cat carrier between me and stacks of munchies on the front passenger seat.

My beautiful Cheyenne lay buried in our backyard, but my folks agreed to bring Blue and Gypsy to New Mexico once I settled down.

I was ready to leave Arkansas.

After a slow road trip, I checked back into a now favorite Motel 6 near the UNM campus, and began my search. Six days of fast food later, we were in a studio apartment, and by early February, I was a clerk in the Biology Department on the UNM campus. Microscopes, mammals, birds, amphibians and the environment made up my new world.

I bought a mobile home, and once settled on a rented 3/4-acre lot, my parents delivered Gypsy—alone. Blue suffered a fatal stroke after I left for New Mexico, and was now buried next to his brother.

Whether the thin air, sunshine, or mysticism inherent in New Mexico, I quickly found myself in my first political movement. A new friend, her teenage son and I took part in Hands Across America, an effort to call attention to hunger in our country. Our position somewhere between Mile Marker 22 and 23 near Gallup, New Mexico, sparked my new beginning.

***

The biologist stood over my desk, travel reimbursement request in hand. Although a hawk specialist, he recently delved into Mexican wolf reintroduction in the Southwest by virtue of a grant.

"Hey Carol, here's my reimbursement request for my trip to White Sands last week. I'll have another one next month too, when I go back to the mountains down there."

I flipped through his papers.

"It looks like everything's here. That's all I need, but I do have a question." I tossed his paperwork on top of the stack cluttering my inbox and looked up at him.

"What's that?"

"Can you use some volunteer help when you go back down there?"

That simple offer consumed the next several years of my life. As president of the Mexican Wolf Coalition of New Mexico, I also served on two environmental committees reporting to the governor, and Defenders of Wildlife sponsored me, along with Coalition presidents from Arizona and Texas, to lobby Congress for three years. I would need that first free trip to Washington, D.C., in the near future.

In spite of hate mail sent to our homes and a fire bomb thrown into the State Land Commissioner's pickup truck, Mexican wolves were successfully released into the wild in 1998.

***

Somehow a hyper jumping bean, and very pregnant, miniature pincher landed on my doorstep. Four puppies later, she went to a rescue group, I found homes for two of her puppies, and two of them, Spats and Nizhoni, stayed with me.

One morning when I stopped to pet Gpysy before letting her outside with the puppies, I looked at her face.

She's gray. I guess I haven't noticed her getting old.

"Come on Gypsy, let's go outside."

Wagging her tail, she followed me out the door to join Spats and Nizhoni in my fenced yard.

That day turned into another late night, putting me home at dusk.

Oh oh, the puppies are outside the fence!

Seeing me pull up, Spats and Nizhoni crawled back into the yard through their escape hole.

Where's Gypsy? Oh my God, I'll bet I know where she is...

I drove my old pickup a block south and turned down the street running parallel with my property. My headlights illuminated her glossy black coat sprawled across the oncoming lane.

Making a U-turn, I stopped on the shoulder and lifted her lifeless body off the pavement. Carrying her to the bed of the truck, every bone in her body crunched as if I held a beanbag.

God damn cars.

I buried her in the back yard—several times. With river-bottom sand and mounds of wild grasses for a yard, Spats and Nizhoni kept digging her up. It never bothered me. I knew she was no longer in that body.

It was the forerunner of another, closer death. My father battled chronic leukemia for a number of years, but had been doing well. Then my mother called saying I needed to come back to Arkansas if I wanted to spend any quality time with him. I left Albuquerque that night and drove straight through to Lincoln.

Within days, it became apparent I was needed there long term. Returning to New Mexico, I picked up my four-legged family, took a leave of absence from the Biology Department and settled into Lincoln for the duration.

He passed away at home on December 4, 1989, with my mother and I holding his hands. I shed no tears. Not ever. I still feel he never left.

Returning to New Mexico in March, I picked up right where I left off, thanks to the Biology Department holding my job for me.

***

It was April when a newly married friend from Oklahoma needed a place to stay for one night to attend the Gathering of Nations Powwow, so I offered my spare bedroom.

Sound asleep late that night, a heavy weight pushed down first the mattress, then spread out over my body.

Hum...what? What!

He was climbing on top of me.

"Get off! Get off me!"

Pinned down, I twisted under him, pushing against his shoulders and screaming "no." Finally understanding I meant it, he climbed off without so much as an apology, and stumbled back into his bedroom. He was snoring within two minutes, while I remained awake the rest of the night coming to terms with how powerless I felt against him.

Maybe having a man around occasionally would be a good thing.

Carol Martindale-Taylor

***

My personal ad brought in a geologist, a manager from the Bureau of Land Management, and a social worker with child protective services. All professionals, all settled and comfortable in their own skins. Sorry, not interested.

One needy man did continue to show up however. When hang-up calls started coming in after returning from Arkansas, I became suspicious.

Ray? No, there's no way he could find me. He wouldn't even know how to begin looking.

One night I answered my phone and heard that familiar lyrical voice. My mother gave him my phone number because she liked him.

I consented to meeting him half way between Arkansas and New Mexico for a weekend, wondering if somehow things might be different. The only difference was a follow-up phone call with a marriage proposal. As much as I thought I still loved him and enjoyed our great sex life, I wanted that life to last a little longer.

Then I made one of those turns again. Well, actually I cranked the hell out of the wheel.

TRAPPED

Volunteering to sell beaded jewelry and key rings for a Native American federal prison inmate landed me a connection with a friend of his in Maryland. He certainly understood what I needed.

After numerous telephone calls and letters, Delonte Taylor sent me his Army discharge papers, prison health records and criminal case documents for safe keeping. In his early 30s and Black, his apparent victimization by the criminal justice system pulled me straight to him.

Maryland does not care if an offender is physically present during the commission of a crime. If you are in the company of the offenders, you are equally as guilty. With the rape victim unable to identify him, and no previous criminal record, Delonte received a 113-year sentence—the court's version of leniency. His two co-defendants each received six life sentences, plus 99 years.

Delonte was no angel. Holding up drug houses for cash and drugs when on his own, he waited outside while his co-defendants robbed what was supposed to be another drug house. It was a private residence with a young woman in it who paid the price.

Is he telling me the truth?

I needed to meet him in person, and thanks to a friend whose father was a retired airline pilot, I flew to Maryland for free.

Six feet tall, slender and with a quick smile, Delonte was

quiet and thoughtful. Interested in everything about the outside world, and noticeably missing the standard prison tattoos and jargon, I was intrigued.

For Christmas in 1992, I drove to Arkansas, picked up my mother, and we headed for Maryland. He even impressed her.

He called me several days after I returned to New Mexico.

"Well, the day you left here, I went back to the dorm and found a guy stealing my food stash."

"Oh no!"

"Anyway, we got into a fight so now we're both in administrative segregation until they figure out what to do with us."

"Are you okay?"

"I am now. He grabbed a metal dust pan though, so my hands really got sliced up. Doc says a tendon in one finger was cut almost clean through."

"Is it healing okay?"

"Yeah, but I was so covered in blood, one of the guys loaned me a T-shirt until I can wash mine."

That bloody? I hope that guy wasn't HIV+.

"Well, hopefully everything gets straightened out soon. Defenders of Wildlife is flying me to Washington in March, to lobby Congress on wolf reintroduction. It would be a perfect time to visit you again."

***

I pounded the halls of Senate and House government buildings for 2-1/2 days, along with the other Coalition presidents, and then stayed over an extra day. After visiting Delonte, I met with a public defender familiar with his case.

The attorney, finished reviewing Delonte's transcripts in preparation for a re-sentencing hearing, kicked back in his chair. I sensed him waiting for my reaction.

"I have to tell you Ms. Martindale, on paper he looks vicious. It was a heinous crime, and I'm sure the woman was never the same after the attack." Leaning forward, he now made no attempt to hide his concern.

"I know, but he told me what happened, and I believe he's

being honest with me."

"Well, I'll tell you this much. After reading the trial transcript, it's obvious his defense attorney didn't give a damn. I can't say he did anything illegal, but he sure didn't care about defending him."

"Yeah, I heard how he didn't even introduce the fact that none of the fingerprints or hair samples belonged to Delonte."

"Well, here." Reaching across his desk, he handed me a massive manila envelope. "All I can do is give you a copy of the transcript. Maybe it will help in some way."

The nearly 400-page trial and sentencing transcript provided in-flight reading on my way home.

How did he ever get convicted of First Degree rape? I'm sure once the courts take another look, they'll see where they screwed up.

***

More time than usual passed before Delonte called again.

"Man, I've been feeling crummy. I've had a fever for several days that the doctors can't explain. Of course, as usual, it's take an aspirin and go back to your cell."

"Are you getting any better?"

"Yeah, it seems to be backing off a little."

"Maybe you're fighting the flu."

"I guess so. Anyway, I feel better than I did yesterday. So what's going on out there?"

"Well, I turned in my notice at work, and will head your way in early July. That'll give me time to sell my trailer and furniture. I'll be bringing Spats, Nizhoni and Sabrina with me too, but at least with this move, I have a place to stay when I get there."

"How'd you manage that?"

"Remember my friend who got me the free plane ticket? Well, his girlfriend in Maryland is moving to New Mexico to be close to him, and she said I can stay with her until I get settled."

"Man, that worked out good. Listen, I've gotta go. I'm not feeling so good again. I'll call before you leave New Mexico."

"Okay. Hope you start feeling better. I'll see you in a couple of months."

He called back a few weeks later.

"I'm in Five Locks being processed through to a new prison, and decided I better call you."

I barely heard his trembling voice. Something was terribly wrong.

"What's up?"

"Remember when I had that high fever, and they couldn't figure out why?"

"Yeah."

"Well, the guy I fought with was HIV positive...and now, so am I."

Dead silence at both ends of the line.

It was a death sentence. The average life expectancy was four years, but only two years for inmates.

What do I say?

"I wanted you to know." His voice faded away.

My racing mind failed to give me anything.

"We'll work on it when I get there," was the best I could manage.

The line went dead.

Coming out of two days in shock, I realized my plans were unchanged.

His call told me everything I needed to know about him. I never would have known his HIV status if he had not told me. A rapist? Not even close.

He wrote telling me where he was being sent and how he felt. I could only say I would see him soon.

After the Fourth of July, with clothes stacked in my car again, Sabrina in her carrier, and Spats and Nizhoni on the back floor, I headed for Maryland. I had a bachelor's degree in anthropology and a few dollars in my pocket. It was time to head east.

***

After the usual 'I'm new in town' disasters, I moved in with Gabe and William in Baltimore.

Gabe, a former student employee I processed into the Biology

Department at UNM, needed one more roommate in her rented row home. She and William were working on their Ph.D.'s at Johns Hopkins, the house was near the University of Baltimore and on the city bus line. A done deal.

I landed a part-time sales job in Baltimore's stylish Inner Harbor, and then a series of contract jobs at the Smithsonian Institution. The fall of 1993 found me enrolled in the University of Baltimore's criminal justice program.

Then Delonte decided he wanted to get married, and although I needed no such paper, I agreed. I knew it would give him some peace of mind in the sense that he could feel he was leading at least a quasi-life with someone who cared about him.

We married on November 17 of 1993, our wedding anniversary forever set by the prison warden. The ceremony was conducted in the prison lobby before visiting hours, and with gold bands I purchased for us. Two correctional officers served as witnesses.

"I wish your father was still alive," my mother commented when I gave her the news over the telephone. When I reminded her that my father would not have judged Delonte, she thought about it for a moment and agreed.

***

One criminal justice class proved to be more interesting than others. When the Executive Director of the National Correctional Industries Association showed up as a guest speaker, I followed her out into the hallway. From there, it was on to a job I loved for the next ten years, one that led to a personal and professional involvement with an international prison reform group.

From the outside, my life appeared settled. Married, although minus one breadwinner, I had a well-paying job I enjoyed, and was making steady progress on my master's degree.

From the inside, it was chaotic and disturbing.

Physically trapped, and knowing he would soon die an agonizing death, Delonte hit a wall. His anger and frustration required an outlet, and who better to unleash it on than his wife?

I was not selected so much as I was the only person in his corner.

"White bitch! I'm just another expendable Black boy!" The voice coming through the telephone shredded me.

I sat there, thoughts jumbled together.

I don't deserve this.

With no family visiting him, even though they lived in the area, and no one else knowing his HIV status, I was his only sounding board.

How much longer can I take this? How much longer should I take this?

Some days, I quietly waited until he calmed down, and then tried for a civil conversation. Occasionally the ploy worked, but not often.

I tried talking about his situation with him other days, but what do you say to someone dying in a trap like the Mexican wolves I fought to reintroduce?

If the telephone calls were gut wrenching, at least our visits were not as volatile. There was no yelling, but more than once, he stood up and walked out on me.

Four times in our first three years together, I planned to move back to New Mexico.

I can send him a few dollars every month, and do it from a safe distance.

Then I imagined him in a small cell every day, serving for all intents and purposes, a life sentence. A place where no one loved him and no one visited him.

I can't leave him. What would he do?

Taking a detour from work on his legal case, I campaigned to get him on the new three-drug regimen available to HIV patients on the outside. Letters and fact sheets to the authorities resulted in a lecture by the state medical officer about how this will mean doing it for all inmates.

When Delonte went on the standard three-drug regime available on the outside, it worked well. His T-cell count rebounded to the 600s, and the viral load became undetectable.

Did I save his life? Maybe. And maybe I saved him so he could stay trapped behind those bars for the rest of it.

ON THE ROAD AGAIN

I visited Delonte twice a week and sent money every month while working on his legal case. Two attorneys became interested in taking his case pro bono, but backed off when they realized his original attorney was now a judge. It was a wise move. When a state's attorney, the friend of a correctional officer who liked Delonte, asked the judge about the case, the judge responded "I'd advise you to drop this."

I kept digging anyway, hoping he survived long enough to come home.

Then it happened again. It was December of 1999, and with our hour visit almost over, I watched Delonte's face as we talked.

He's gray! His face is gray!

Struggling to stay focused on our conversation, I was grateful when the officer signaled it was time for me to leave.

The next morning, Gypsy's gray face and Delonte's flashed back and forth. I told a co-worker what happened in the hope talking about it would somehow prevent a catastrophe.

My phone rang at 10:00 p.m. on December 19, 1999, a quiet Sunday evening, and the caller identified himself as a correctional officer who knew both of us. He could have been fired for making direct contact with me.

"Hello. Is this Mrs. Taylor?"

"Yes, I'm Mrs. Taylor."

"This is Officer Smith from the Jessup prison. I have a nurse here who wants to talk to you."

My heart skipped a beat.

Unending muffled sounds of the phone being handed over to someone else came through the line.

"Mrs. Taylor, this is Nurse Gilbert at Shock Trauma in Baltimore. Mr. Taylor was attacked earlier tonight. He's alive, but in serious condition here in the prison ward. We're on the 6th floor if you want to visit."

"I'm on my way!" The receiver dropped into its cradle.

Forty-five minutes later, the officer at the prison ward's front desk explains I cannot visit until Delonte's official visitors list arrives. Pacing the hospital floor until 1:00 a.m. produced nothing, so I headed home for a few sleepless hours.

Head spinning in my unreal world the next morning, I walked the prison ward hallway looking for him. The sight dropped me to my knees.

Semi-conscious, he labored for each breath. Bright red flesh bordered bandages barely covering seared skin.

Stabbed five times in the upper body, one blade puncturing his left lung, an attacker then threw a full pot of heated baby oil over him. Creating first, second and third degree burns down the left side of his head and neck, the sizzling oil pooled in the concave above his collarbone, cooking flesh.

How could someone hate him this much?

Over the next few days, he pieced together the story.

It started out a typical night. With a towel wrapped around his waist, he left his wristwatch and wedding ring on his bunk, and headed for the dorm showers.

He remembered hearing the verbal signal used when something is going to happen in the showers, warning those not involved to stay away. Mentally miles away however, and not expecting trouble himself, he neglected to give it serious thought.

Walking in, he saw two inmates showering with their backs to him, and one stall door closed. Setting his towel aside, he turned the shower on and stood with his back to the room while adjusting the water temperature.

The two inmates, rags now covering their faces, cornered him between them and the wall. Thrusting long prison-made shanks into his chest, a third attacker stepped out from the closed stall, and tossed the pot of heated baby oil over him.

Wet feet slipping on cement, Delonte dodged slashing blades the best he could while fighting his way to the exit. Throwing his weight into the door, it did not budge. A fourth unseen inmate trapped him inside.

Dropping to the floor with multiple stab wounds apparently convinced his attackers their job was done. They calmly walked out of the shower.

Finally able to get on his feet, Delonte watched bloody bubbles pump out of his chest as he staggered into the dorm. Leaving a trail of blood behind him, he stumbled down the aisle toward the officer's desk at the front of the dorm, and seconds before passing out, heard an inmate call for help.

With dense fog preventing a Life Flight helicopter from landing at the prison, a local ambulance rushed him to an outside hospital. Inmates and officers alike assumed he was a dead man.

***

Days later, he was transferred to the prison infirmary, where the medical staff missed seeing his prescription for pain medication by the hospital's doctor. They gave him aspirin instead, and continually forgot his HIV medications.

After release from the infirmary, his next stop was administrative segregation while the incident was investigated. For the first time, we visited through plexiglass. We would need to get used to it.

"I'm not going to let fear dictate what I do. I'm going to press charges against them," he told me over the visiting room telephone.

"I had even been trying to help the White dude—the one with the hot pot. I know one of the Black guys because he bunks near me, and I know the other one is in a gang. The only one I don't know is whoever held the door shut from the outside."

"Will they come after you?"

"That's okay. I'll go into Protective Custody and stay there. It's the only way. It's more restrictive, but I can't let them get away with this. I think the whole thing happened because one of my co-defendants called out a hit on me."

An inmate filing criminal charges against another inmate is admirable. A death wish, but admirable.

After the State Police and courts worked through everything, the 'hot pot attacker' received 11 additional years, but no charges were brought against the gang member or the inmate bunking near him. Several inmates were listed as possible attackers, so the investigators decided Delonte did not know who attacked him, even though he was not the one who created the list. My own research revealed the State ran out of money to prosecute inmate-on-inmate attacks.

The physical injuries healed, but the emotional ones refused. In the middle of the night, he punched the air and the wall along his bunk. The prison psychiatrist put him on anti-anxiety medication, but there was no therapy for what appeared to be post-traumatic stress disorder.

Eventually life returned to our normal, with the addition of plexiglass. Our marriage smoothed out, I completed my master's degree in criminal justice and had a job I loved.

Well, I thought I did.

In 2005, our office lost 84% of its Federal grant funding. We let half of our staff go, and those left took tremendous cuts in salary—$28,000 a year in my case—plus changes in job duties. I stuck it out for one more year.

Resigning from the National Correctional Industries Association after ten years, I assumed taking my Social Security benefit, minus the early withdrawal penalty, would be balanced out by finding work elsewhere.

That was when I discovered I was old.

No one told me I was old. It dawned on me when employment agencies never called me about jobs, even though I scored high on their tests and had good interviews. One agent openly admitted age discrimination was living and well.

I knew spending money unnecessarily would soon be on a back burner, so of course that was when I saw something I could not resist. In a Sunday newspaper in 2006, there was an article about Allyson Walsh, a respected psychic medium living six miles from me. I wanted a reading by a reputable psychic since Cliff's mother went to one in Phoenix.

Allyson was good. She brought up the names of relatives, and insisted Delonte recently received something to help him walk, while I insisted he had not. Weeks passed before I remembered the knee brace a prison doctor gave him.

As my reading came to a close that July day, I asked Allyson one final question.

"By the way, did a boy friend of mine come through? He was killed in a car wreck years ago."

"No, no one like that came through."

"Okay. I was just wondering."

***

With time on my hands, and my entire four-legged family now living over the 'rainbow bridge,' I decided to volunteer at a local cat rescue while job hunting.

The owner did not need another volunteer. She needed someone to mop all six floors, clean litter boxes, and feed and medicate 50 cats. Would I be interested in such a hard, dirty job?

I asked when I could start.

The cats staved off starvation until early 2008, when my savings account became a figment of my imagination. The next move would be into my 1996 Buick.

Delonte was on stable emotional footing by then, and some of his family started visiting occasionally. Thankfully, he understood my survival meant a drastic change.

March of 2008, found me cruising I-40 West back to Arkansas.

LIFE AS A GHOST HUNTER

Eleven hundred miles later, I turned north into northwest Arkansas and the duplex where my mother now lived.

Arriving in her parking lot in Prairie Grove, a small town seven miles east of my former home in Lincoln, my wallet was the proud owner of 50 cents. Relying on Social Security with plans to find a local job, I expected a financial recovery in six months and a move back to Maryland.

Once settled into a temp job in nearby Fayetteville, I began a routine of walking the quarter-mile track across the street from us. Ever watchful, one morning I noticed a white pickup truck parked in an adjacent lot, and facing the track.

After I completed another trip around the track, the truck pulled out on a parallel road, moved onto a cross street and drove away.

I would have felt relief if the driver had not looked like Ray. Two more trips around the track, and I walked home.

"Hi, honey. Hey, Ray just called here." My mother smiled.

"What?"

He figured out I wasn't in Maryland by calling my old phone number!

"Yeah, he asked how you were doing. He left his phone number for you to call him."

"Like that's going to happen."

Two hang-up calls and one "hi" recorded message later, I had an idea.

"Hello," answered the familiar voice.

"Hi Ray, it's Carol. How ya doing?"

"Great! I figured you moved back here. How long have you been in town?"

"Just a few weeks now. Hey, how about meeting me at McDonalds in Farmington? We could get caught up. It's been a long time."

"Sure. Would tomorrow morning around 11:30 work?"

"Sounds good. I'll see you there."

What better way to dissolve his fantasy than confronting it with reality?

Although small talk over an unfinished meal the next day was the best we could manage, I hoped it broke the spell.

An occasional "hello" still found its way to our telephone recorder for a while, but then through a chance meeting with his now grown daughter, I learned he was recovering from a stroke. I sent him my best wishes.

***

With steady paychecks coming in from the temp agency, I allowed myself to relax. First I joined the Arkansas Archeological Society, and then I hunted for a group active in another interest.

Decades of reading about the paranormal made a believer out of me, although I never experienced anything myself. Death premonitions, seeing gray 'death masks' and a sensation of sadness failed to qualify, probably because I never saw the requisite ghost.

Thanks to multiple paranormal TV shows, I caught a serious case of ghost hunter-itis.

Fishing for a local group on the internet one night, the website for Arkansas Paranormal Investigations (API) appeared. An e-mail to Alan, its founder, wrangled me an invitation to their next investigation.

It was mid-August, and API was investigating a relatively

new house in nearby Farmington. The bright red pickup truck towing a 16-foot-long trailer wrapped in white, blue and purple lightning bolts, made the place easy to find. They also made it easy for the entire neighborhood and local police, who continually cruised by, to suspect a haunted house existed in their midst.

With the back doors of the trailer propped open, a handful of people marched back and forth between it and the front door of the house. Each carried card tables, computer equipment and bags of what I learned were hand-held electronics.

"Hi, I'm Carol. Where can I find Alan?"

A tall, lanky blond juggled a microphone stand in one hand and three folded tripods in the other. She nodded toward a man walking into the rear of the trailer.

"Hi, and that's Alan." She continued her act, deftly navigating the steps at the client's front door.

"Thanks," I called over my shoulder as I neared the trailer.

"Hi Alan. I'm Carol."

"Hey, glad you could make it. We can always use extra hands. Go on inside and look for a short blonde. She'll tell you where help is needed. Nice to meet you."

"Great. Nice to meet you too."

Picking my way over extension cords strung across living room carpet, I nearly crashed into the obvious 'short blond' heading back outside.

"Oops, sorry. I'm Carol. Alan said to ask you where you need help."

"Good. Out in the trailer you'll see a collection of small white cameras. Grab four and bring them inside."

"Sure."

Half a dozen trips later, Alan and I stood outside the client's master bedroom closet. Eyes fixed on the closed door in front of us, we listened to the growl coming from behind it.

Not only was I hooked, I discovered that like most other paranormal investigators, I found nothing scary about being onsite during an investigation. People frightened by things going bump in the night usually sign up for a touristy ghost hunt out of curiosity, but that is all. The rest of us are fascinated by the possibilities offered, and the opportunity to help those who are truly frightened by what is happening around them. We want answers.

API members caravanned when needed, and traveled in the truck when lucky. With 'Ghost Hunter' written in glowing letters on its doors and the trailer hitched to it, road trips were magical.

Over the years, we investigated the Bird Cage Theatre in Tombstone, the Castle Rock Inn in Bisbee, Miss Molly's B&B in Fort Worth and the Titanic Exhibit in Branson, Missouri. After investigating numerous homes and businesses across Arkansas, our solid reputation meant all three local television stations did stories on us, or with us, multiple times over the years.

My first seven years as a paranormal investigator confirmed I am not sensitive to other worldly beings. The most I could muster might be a hunch on whether or not an area was active. As for sensing deceased loved ones nearby, those things happened to our clients, never me.

Although not a sensitive, or maybe because of it, I developed a reputation as a 'debunker' for API. Smelling and looking like a rose does not automatically make something a rose, not even a ghostly one.

That does not mean I lacked paranormal experiences out in the field. Something unseen grabbed the back of my T-shirt during one investigation, and I heard a disembodied woman's voice next to me during another case. Asked by the public if such things frighten us, our standard answer is no, they do not. It happens so fast, there is no time to shriek or run; it is a "wow, that was interesting" moment. Capturing unheard voices on recorders, or watching orbs return to a camera lens to fly around it a few times before flying off again, become common place occurrences.

One early incident I did not record however, would come back to haunt me—pardon the pun—in 2017.

It happened on a Monday morning in 2008, after my third investigation with API. Taking my mother to her sales job, I returned home to find our porch light on.

That's weird. I hope there's not a wiring problem.

Unlocking the front door, I looked above the high-backed chair in front of the light switch. The switch had been flipped to the 'on' position.

I wonder if Mom turned it on for some reason.

I doubted it because like me, she never used that light.

Well, I'll ask her. If she didn't use it, I'll test it tomorrow.

As we left to run errands the next morning, I made sure the light was off and the door locked.

When we returned minutes later, we found the light switch flipped on again.

Something must have followed me home after that last investigation. Well, that'll teach me to speak up when we forget to say our closing prayer for protection.

As time passed, between ghost hunting, archeology and a new part-time job at the local senior center, I created a comfortable routine for myself. Then my long dormant interest in writing could no longer resist exposing itself.

THE MANUSCRIPT

I always enjoyed writing, so after completing an assortment of writing classes over the years, I jumped into the field beginning in 2011. With the successful publication of a handful of short magazine articles, another old nagging urge returned.

It sprang up during the fall of 2013, with the 50th anniversary of Dave's death looming large on July 10 of the next year. Long wanting to put his story down on paper, and assuming it would be good therapy, I decided to start the project in time for completion by July 10, 2014. I would honor his memory on his birthday.

Pulling duffle bags crammed with old photos out of the closet, I sat in the middle of my bedroom floor, dumping their contents around me. Fanning stacks into massive poker hands, I found those I needed. Dave alone, us together, us with friends.

Scanned and saved on my computer, the originals went into a little blue album, and I started work on a magazine article.

I began noticing things.

I did not remember Dave wearing his class ring on his left hand. Details of a huge beach party Alice and I put together were gone. The address of the apartment where my life changed forever was gone.

Yet I did remember reaching for his hand when we posed for the picture taken during our dinner party in March of 1964. I remembered being unable to stand close to him, and not touch him. I remembered how we never talked about love, yet it overpowers everything in our pictures together.

For the first time ever, I realized we were engaged at the time of his death. When he said we were probably a little too young to make plans to get married right then and I agreed, it was his proposal and my acceptance. The only thing missing was a date. Did I subconsciously block that out all these years? Would the realization at that time have sent me over the edge?

I struggled to write. The right words were elusive at best, heartbreaking at worst. What I assumed would be good therapy turned into something else. I dusted off all the old feelings and explored them, some buried so deep they had never seen the light of day.

And that was the problem.

On November 6, 1964, I should have wrapped myself in grief and worked my way through it. Instead, I carried on with life. Four months of not knowing why he left me, kept me 'out there,' and I believed that world had to go on "with a stiff upper lip."

Now, after dinner and dishes every night, I closed myself in my bedroom, flipped on the computer and worked on the article. The words should have flowed, but they were not there. I studied each picture, hoping memories made words appear on blank pages. I wrote paragraph after paragraph, lining through most.

Finally creating a manuscript of sorts for submission, it was promptly rejected. When efforts to revise it in a meaningful way failed week after week, I questioned whether I even wanted it in a magazine. It felt too trite, too short a venue to do him justice.

Somewhere in the mix, a thought came to me. Although his sister and I stayed in contact for a time after his death, life happened, and we went our separate ways.

Maybe she would like to read the story.

An internet search produced a likely address, and after mailing her a letter, she called me. Yes, she wanted to read the magazine story.

The manuscript landed in her e-mail on July 5, 2014, the 50th anniversary of the last time Dave and I were together. Within days, her e-mailed response starting with "I'm sitting here with tears streaming down my face..." arrived. Like most young men of that era, writing letters home was not a big priority, so she never knew what those last few weeks were like for her big brother. Now she could fill in the blanks.

After exchanging messages with her and putting publication attempts on hold, everything came to a halt. All I had left were fresh, re-opened wounds, and memories half a century old.

I began closing myself in my bedroom every night again. This time, a click on my desktop opened Dave's photos. A second click sent the slide show function into action. When the steady stream of pictures was not enough, I hit the pause button on favorite frames. When no longer satisfied with that, I brought up favorites individually, increasing them until each was life size. With his eyes so close to mine, I felt him with me.

Along with each picture came the tears. It did not take them long to start, and they started every night. I physically ached. I wanted to feel him touch me again, feel him sitting against my right thigh.

Other memories flooded back. Memories of threatening to tweeze the tuft of chest hair peeking up over his undershirt, of him in the passenger seat of my old Mercury, of him in my parent's spare bedroom surrounded by yellow bed sheets.

I realized he never smiled in posed pictures because of his chipped front tooth, so pictures of him laughing became special.

In pictures taken at the beach the last weekend in June of 1964, he is wrapped around me, as if protecting me. I imagined him sheltering me again. In the very last picture of him ever taken, we are huddled together on the beach, and for the first time, I noticed the long shadow stretching across the sand behind us.

Maneuvering around the Internet brought up pictures of his

headstone in Dublin, Georgia, and the *Mahan* steaming into a port in Japan in February of 1964. The white captain's gig is visible suspended over the deck. Dave appeared in a group photograph taken on board the ship during that cruise.

I dissolved into heavier tears thinking about what we never had together.

No man ever looked at me the way he did in front of Mission de Alcala and during our dinner party. So much could have been, that would never be.

Every night during the early summer of 2014, decades of unspent grief poured out from some unknown depth. I told no one about my private hell. No one would understand.

I didn't save him.

I could've saved him.

If I had said yes to sex, his feelings wouldn't have been as intense, and he would have stayed with his friends in Long Beach that night. What was the big deal about virginity anyway? It sure doesn't mean anything now.

Sitting on the edge of my bed late one night re-reading the manuscript, I realized what I had done.

I didn't save Dave so I found other men to save!

IS IT REALLY YOU?

A neighbor and API team member house sits as a side business, so when she saw an apparition at the home of a client, she obtained permission for us to conduct a 'mini' investigation. It was late July, and I needed the diversion.

Sitting in the den with the lights out, I switched on my voice recorder while she fired up a new ghost hunting app on her cell phone.

"Hi, my name is Myrna. Is there anyone here who would like to talk to us?"

Silence.

"Hi, I'm Carol. We don't want to scare you, we just want to find out who is here."

She tried again. "If someone is here, can you give us your name?"

"David," said the cell phone.

"Oh, that reminds me," I chimed in, "I finally finished that manuscript I've been working on about Dave. I probably won't try to publish it, but at least it brought his sister and me back together after all these years."

Minutes passed in silence when further questioning produced no responses.

"Well, there's sure not much going on in here. Maybe we should try another room," I suggested.

"Yeah, let's go into the kitchen."

Our move into the kitchen produced a broken wind-up clock

suddenly ticking again, but nothing else, so we called it a night.

Two weeks later, on a nondescript Sunday afternoon, I left the Farmington McDonald's where I often did my writing, and ran errands on my way home.

After a quick trip into a local grocery store, I returned to my car, lowered both front windows and eased across the empty parking lot.

Brrr...ring.

What? Did I forget to turn off my cell phone?

Stopping in the middle of the huge lot, I dug the phone out of my handbag.

Yep, it's off, but I know I heard it ring. Oh, I'll bet that car passing me had the same ring tone and I heard it through the open window. Yeah, that's what happened.

Throwing the contraption back into the abyss that was the bottom of my purse, I entered the main road and headed for a Dollar Store in Prairie Grove.

Ten minutes later, I parked the car, slipped my handbag over my left shoulder and walked into the store. Finding an assortment of candy and chips, I soon stood behind two other customers waiting to be checked out.

Brrr...ring. Brrr...ring.

What in the world? It rang twice this time. I'm positive I turned it off.

Positive or not, once back in my car, I rummaged through my purse again.

Yep, it's off.

Arriving at home, I headed for the landline phone in my bedroom.

"Hey, you're not going to believe this," I blurted out to my API neighbor as I pulled my desk chair close to the phone.

"Why? What?"

"I think something followed me home from our last investigation. Two times on my way home a few minutes ago, my cell phone rang while it was turned off. At first I thought it came from a passing car, but the second time, I was standing in line at the Dollar store. My handbag was inches away under my left arm."

"Well, they like messing with electronics. Maybe it's something from that big shop we did a few weeks ago."

"Yeah, or that last client up in Bella Vista. Well, I'll see what happens."

A week later, my mother and I stood in the kitchen fixing sandwiches for a quick dinner. After throwing ham and sliced cheese on a couple pieces of wheat bread, I headed for my usual spot on the sofa. It was time for the 6:00 p.m. news.

Resting my plate on the coffee table, I adjusted the volume on the remote, then reached for the plate.

My hand stopped in midair.

What in the...Dave? You're here! I know you're right here!

I ran my hand over a spot on the sofa along my right thigh.

You're next to me. I know you're right next to me.

I froze, not in fear, but in disbelief. I was thinking about my rumbling stomach and that sandwich, yet suddenly I knew he was next to me on my right side, exactly where he would have been in life.

The sensation soon faded away.

During my seven years of ghost hunting, I never gave much credence to people feeling the presence of deceased loved ones, yet I 'felt' him against me.

Then I remembered 'David' coming through a cell phone app, and my own cell phone ringing two different times while it was turned off.

Oh hell!

I analyzed everything. First it was all coincidence, then it was Dave coming through, then it was wishful thinking.

In mid-October, I attended a writers' conference in Eureka Springs, Arkansas. Opting to drive over Friday morning, I rented a room for two nights, and planned to drive home Sunday morning. My voice recorder and camera landed in my suitcase before my clothes.

Although exhausted after spending all day in workshops,

Saturday night I set up my equipment. Having no luck with the voice recorder, I switched to my camera and snapped dozens of pictures around my motel room. Then I asked for a favor.

"Okay Dave, if you're really here with me, please try to give me an orb. I'm sorry I doubt it really is you, but please try to show me an orb."

An orb appeared over my bed.

Walking around the room photographing the walls, the bed and the floor, nothing else showed up.

"I'm sorry to ask again, but I'm so unsure about whether or not you are here. Can you please show me an orb again?"

Another orb appeared over the bed.

Sunday morning when I repeated my request, another orb appeared. Out of 160 pictures taken, orbs appeared in seven, and only when I asked for them.

Things like this don't happen to me.

Although still feeling a strong sense of his presence, as an investigator with a reputation for debunking, I needed more proof. Days later, I tried another experiment.

"Okay babe," I said out loud late one night, "if it is you, please give me something about Old Spice. Not seeing it in the store, because I see it there all the time. Please give me something special about Old Spice so I'll know it really is you."

The next night, I repeated my request.

Around 3:00 that morning, I woke and was unable to go back to sleep. Turning on my computer, I checked e-mail and looked for the latest news.

An article appeared about an inmate being released after serving decades for a crime he did not commit. With my masters in criminal justice and Delonte's current predicament, I kept up on such proceedings so I clicked on the article.

For the offender's last crime before incarceration, he stole a handful of small items, including two sticks of Old Spice deodorant.

My last inhale refused to exhale. I stared at the screen.

What am I supposed to do now?

Shortly before Christmas, another type of incident happened that I often questioned. How can spirits send a song with special meaning when you need it most?

Returning to the senior center after making our bank deposit one afternoon, and deep in thought about the possibilities unfolding around Dave, I heard Anastasia sing "you will never be alone" over my car radio. Goosebumps covered me while listening to it, so I located the lyrics and video on line that night.

It is a love story about a young woman leaving her boyfriend's home late one evening, and crashing her car to avoid hitting a wolf. Her spirit runs back to her boyfriend for help and he rescues her.

A young couple, a car crash, a spirit—and a wolf? Perhaps spirits influence us to be listening when we most need it...

Several mornings later while lying in bed mentally running through my day's schedule, bunched-up bedding pressed down on my right hip, the sensation traveling across my lower back and fading out as it reached my left hip.

Oh my God! Is he touching me?

More days of wonder and doubts passed.

At work late one afternoon, Bobby Hatfield of the Righteous Brothers came over the radio singing 'Unchained Melody.' Always reminding me of Dave, I added it to my collection of our songs.

Then a thought struck me.

Maybe I should call that psychic medium in Maryland. Allyson Walsh is good and I trust her.

I decided it was time. I tracked down Allyson on the internet, and although I could not afford her fee, I did notice that she gave readings over the telephone. I knew she allowed clients to record her sessions, so if I did this, I would need to buy a telephone with a speaker.

Worried about the expense, I looked for a local reputable psychic, but internet searches and appeals to friends were unsuccessful. Armed with only wishful thinking, around 1:00 a.m. on Monday, Dec. 29, I looked at Allyson's website again.

Finished reading through it, I clicked on a link to watch an orb she filmed during her visit to the Cashtown Inn near Gettysburg. At the end of the short video, a square collage containing four links popped up on my monitor.

One linked to Bobby Hatfield singing 'Unchained Melody.'
Okay, I'll find the damn money!

THE READING

I dreaded calling Allyson. The more I looked at Dave's pictures and thought about him, the more terrified I became he would not 'come through.' Maybe it was because the last time I waited for him, he did not show up. Maybe because I still had trouble believing all these signs were really from him. They could be coincidence, or the product of an over-active imagination. They could even be just wishful thinking.

But the possibility that he sat next to me, was back in my life again, brought me tears of joy.

I spent days bouncing between fear, anticipation, memories and back to fear. Throwing caution to the wind one day, and with a pounding heart, I called Allyson.

We scheduled a telephone reading for Saturday, January 17, 2015, at 1:00 p.m. She talked about listing five questions for whoever I hoped would come through, but I never mentioned Dave or even a former boyfriend.

That list of questions assumed a life of its own. It instantly became an open letter to him, with thoughts meant for him alone. It also became a diary for me, an extension of my psyche.

I spent days vacillating between peace knowing it was going to happen, and all-consuming fear knowing it was going to happen.

Is it all my imagination? Is it all a series of coincidences? Maybe he really is here, but won't come through.

Saturday afternoon, with a new speaker phone and two voice recorders running, I dialed Allyson's telephone number.

"Hello."

"Hi Allyson, it's Carol."

"Hi, Carol. How have you been?"

"Great. Hey, it's good to talk with you again. You know, my last reading was in 2006."

"Yeah, it's been a long time."

"Listen, the main reason I wanted to have a reading with you…I did something last July, and since I did it, I've had a whole raft of things happen. I keep thinking they're not coincidence, but they might be wishful thinking. I don't know. I just don't know."

"Let me ask you something. Are you having what we call physical phenomena happen in your house?"

"There was one incident. I was sitting on the sofa one night two or three months ago, and I could have sworn this person was sitting right next to me."

"Well, I'll tell you something. I don't think it's totally over yet. I mean, I think you may be having that happen again."

"Okay, that's interesting you say that. About four or five weeks ago, I got out of bed to go to the bathroom, got back in bed and rolled over on my left side. I remember the blankets were bunched up over my right hip. You know sometimes when bedding is heavy, how it will kind of relax and fall? This felt like a pressure pushing it down, and then it went down my back to my left hip."

"Yeah, I felt like maybe somebody was trying to make their presence known by putting pressure on something."

"I actually started doing an open letter to this person because I've had so many things happen."

"Let me ask you, is this a man you are writing the letter to?"

"Yeah. Matter of fact, when I saw you in 2006, I asked if my boyfriend who died came through, but he hadn't. I think it was because I wasn't ready."

"Oh, all right."

"What happened in this case, I'd been wanting to write a story about what happened with us, and..."

"Now somebody is singing like a child's song to me that I remember from many years ago. John Jacob Jinkleheimer Schmidt, and I keep seeing the letter 'J'. A letter 'J' that looks kind of like fish hooks dancing in my head. Do you have somebody whose name is like..."

"James?"

"The song was like John Jacob Jingleheimer Schmidt, his name is my name too. Is there like a John, Joe, or Jim or James somebody?"

"James. James David Alligood."

No, I can't get my hopes up.

"James?"

"James David Alligood," I repeated.

"That's who it is."

"Okay. Okay. That's who I..."

"Is he the one you wrote the letter to?"

"Yes."

"That's who's here right now. And yes, he says you've been feeling...my god, my hair's standing up.

"So is mine!"

Is he really here?

"You've been feeling the pressure. As if he like sat down, or was in the bed, or...see what I'm saying?"

"I had the feeling he was on the sofa. He always used to sit on my right side when we visited with my parents, and I had the feeling he was sitting right there. I froze. I just froze."

"Really?"

"It wasn't because I was afraid. I just couldn't believe what I was feeling, and then in a few seconds it went away. But I've had other things happen too. It's like those instances we talk about in ghost hunting when people have unfinished business."

I launched into the story of his death in 1964, and how it always felt like unfinished business.

"As you were talking, I've now seen this several times. I was being shown a single rose, as if a hand is holding one single stemmed rose. Did he ever bring you a rose?"

"No."

"Or the name Rose. Is that significant? I'm wondering if Dave is trying to show you something about a rose, or if it's somebody by the name of Rose."

"Not that I remember."

"Now is something important...I don't know why I'm hearing this, but is something important about the month of May?"

"Now, we met in May of 1963."

"All right, I've still got him here then. He was trying to bring that up because there was something commemorative about it."

"Yeah, a mutual friend introduced us. We had a really interesting relationship. We never questioned each other, and eventually let everyone else go until it was just the two of us. Of course, our open relationship left me not knowing for a long time what had happened to him. I'm in touch with his sister now, and..."

"I've heard this twice now. Would there be more than one James, or more than one David, in his family? Would you know that?"

"No, but I could find out. I don't know what his Dad's name was because they were not close."

"Okay. Find out for me. Sometimes when they float something past me, I like to wait until I hear it again, and I've heard it again now. I think he's trying to bring somebody else through from his family."

"Okay. I can find out."

"Does the name William or Bill mean something to you?"

"Oh, I've probably known two or three Bills."

"All right, I'm also getting that name coming in too, but I feel that this is for you."

"Interesting."

"I think that he's definitely around you a lot right now."

"This William or Dave?"

"He is definitely trying to make an impression," she laughed.

"Who's that? Which one?"

"I say David. He's definitely trying to…I mean sometimes I wonder about them. They'll visit us, but then leave and later come back. I don't try to analyze it any more. It might happen when they have time to look in on us."

"A friend and I talked about this last night. About how you can't get a command performance. You have to go with whatever spirits come through."

"Now the photographs you're taking. I tell you what, I've been impressed upon it again for a second time. You might want to take some of those photographs you have taken in your bedroom, and look at them on the computer. I think you may be getting a face of David."

"Okay."

"I think you are going to have something more show up in these orbs."

I need to know.

"Allyson, will he and I see each other in the future?"

"I think there is going to be some kind of what I call materialization. That you may actually see either an outline of him, or maybe more like a transparency with some ectoplasm or something of him. Is that what you're talking about?"

"Yeah, or well, in the future."

"Are you talking about on the Other Side?"

"Either, or, in the future."

"Yeah, I think you are. I think part of the reason why he's around you right now is he was trying to show me your chemistry is changing, meaning you are becoming more kind of mediumistic. He's going to try to show himself to you now that you've picked up on the fact that you know it's him. And the fact that you are with this paranormal group, doing all the things that are right in being able to communicate. That you even know it's him when you ask for proof. I'm telling you, I know it's going to happen. It's not going to happen when you expect it, but believe me, he's going to make more than a pressure. It's going to be more of a presence."

"Okay."

"But yeah, he is saying that you will…that he'll be there for you when you come over. But you're not coming over any time soon."

Thank you babe, thank you!

"That was the main thing."

"Is your mother in her 90s?"

"Yes, 92."

"Okay. For some reason he was showing me something important about the number 93 with her."

"Her birthday's coming up in April."

"All right. Now, did he meet her long ago?"

"Yeah."

"He wanted to say hello to her, and that he was trying to let me know that she was going to be 93 this year. It was another verification that it is him."

"Okay. Yeah, my folks really liked him. They both really liked him. My poor dad was the one who had to break the news to me."

"Oh, that is so sad."

"By the way, do you have time for one more question?"

"Sure."

"I had a friend at the University of New Mexico, and although we ran around together, it wasn't like we were as close as sisters or anything like that. But since she died, I've realized I miss her more than any of my other friends who have passed away, friends that I'd had for years. Did we have any kind of a relationship before we met?"

"Dave tells me you two are from the same soul group, that you knew her on the Other Side. She was what I call tangenting onto your group. That's a soul who sort of visits another soul group."

"I was wondering about soul groups. That explains a lot. Well, I guess that's about it then."

"It's been great talking with you again, Carol. Maybe we'll be able to work together on a paranormal TV show concept I have in mind. We'll see."

"Well, thanks Allyson, it's been fun. And tell Dave I'll be seeing him."

"I will. Bye."

"Bye."

Saturday, January 17, 2015. The purest, most joyous day of my life.

MEMORY LANE

1963/64

Dave's studio portrait taken shortly before the *USS Mahan* left San Diego for the Western Pacific on August 6, 1963.

Carol Martindale-Taylor

A penny for your thoughts. Was he questioning his decision? August 4, 1963.

Lost in the moment until Bob yelled "Hey, over here!" Overlooking the Pacific Ocean near San Diego, on August 4, 1963.

Bob, Dave and a calico kitten scrambling for her freedom. Mission de Alcala, San Diego. August 4, 1963.

A silent goodbye in front of Mission de Alcala in San Diego, on August 4, 1963.

Carol Martindale-Taylor

Hey, it's a white purse--it will go with either of our outfits! Having fun in front of Mission de Alcala, San Diego, on August 4, 1963.

Souvenirs from a fight while on the *USS Mahan* in the Western Pacific, 1963/64--a cut over Dave's left eye and swollen nose.

On board the *USS Mahan*, Western Pacific, 1963/64. Ronnie (last name unknown) and Dave.

Our formal dinner party after the *USS Mahan* returned to San Diego in March of 1964. Bob, Alice, myself and Dave.

Dave watching me while I talk with him about calling his mother during our dinner party. March of 1964.

Donnie Casey and Dave while visiting Donnie's parents in Dallas. June of 1964.

Bob and Dave work to start a fire for our beach party. June 27, 1964.

Bob eating while Alice watches Dave battle a marshmallow. June 27, 1964.

Dave supervising the installation of a marshmallow on a clothes hanger. That night, we talked about getting married. June 27, 1964.

Laughing after I stuffed marshmallows in his mouth on June 27, 1964. This was the last picture taken of Dave.

ORBS
2014/15

Oct. 11, 2014, in my motel room. Note the orb in the upper right quadrant. It appeared after I asked Dave to show me one if he was present.

On Feb. 26, 2015, this orb appeared in my mother's bedroom. The photo was taken from my bedroom and specifically while I was looking for orbs. Intuition?

Carol Martindale-Taylor

A second photo of the same orb in the photo above. Note its size and position at the top center of the picture; it was moving toward me.

LETTER TO DAVE
JANUARY 17 TO MARCH 13, 2015

Dear Dave:

Sat., Jan. 17, 2015. You did it! I was so afraid it would not happen, but you did it. I cannot begin to tell you what it means to know you are here with me, and that you will be waiting for me on the Other Side.

Please, please keep letting me know you are around. I will try to make you proud.

No terror now. Only peace.

Mon., Jan. 19, 2015. Did you hear me call you a ghost today? There is your world and there is mine, and they only partially mix at random times. I guess we need to lead these separate lives. There will come a time when I will be a ghost too, and it will just be us again; well, us and whoever else is on your side.

Tue., Jan. 20, 2015. I get a whole different feeling looking at your pictures now. A deeper, peaceful feeling, and they bring a smile to my face.

Should I apologize for getting married and having boyfriends? I feel funny about that, knowing you are here.

I wonder if Deacon had called me on July 11, 1964, to tell me what happened, what I would have done. I cannot imagine wanting to live.

Thu., Jan. 22, 2015. I cannot abandon Delonte. It would kill him, but if I out live him, he will be the last man in my life. Knowing you will be there for me in the end is all the comfort I need for the rest of this life.

Wed., Jan. 28, 2015. I spent time tonight feeling terribly alone and missing you. Is that how it is going to be if you leave again? I will need to hold on to the thought that you will be there for me when I cross over. Or maybe you can stay until it is time for me to leave. No one living really knows how this works.

Thu., Jan. 29, 2015. In Bob's Christmas card, he asked if I heard from anyone in California. I wonder if he will believe I have, and one of them was you?
Today I felt you slipping away, yet tonight, I feel you here, and it is so good again.

Mon., Feb. 16, 2015. I cannot believe how naive I was to not realize you could be taken away. I am so sorry it never occurred to me I would need to remember your every word, your every touch.
I wonder if we will physically be together again in the future. Will we be friends, or family, or have a chance as lovers again? We were not lovers in what most people think of in the physical sense, but we were still lovers.

Thu., Feb. 26, 2015. Sometimes I feel you have left, but when I am driving, I often get the strongest sense you are riding shotgun with me.
I photographed an orb in Mom's bedroom earlier today. You or Dad?

Fri., Mar. 13, 2015. After you died, I never shed another tear over the death of anyone, including my father; I was a daddy's girl too. It was like a faucet turned off.

    Love,
    Carol

A LIGHT ON THE SUBJECT

After 245,000 miles, you think I would have given it a name, but I still was not sure if it was a 'she' or a 'he.' Faithful to a fault however, my 1996 Buick did have its erratic moments. In early April of 2015, my automatic headlights were no longer automatic. In fact, at times they were not headlights at all.

Driving a mere two blocks on either bumpy or glass-smooth roads, they snapped off and on. I knew driving at night would mean guessing the location of potholes and praying for a center dividing line. Experimenting with the manual override still left me driving without lights, so with no money to support our local mechanic, I developed 'The Plan.'

The Plan was simple—do not drive after dark. Believing as I often did that something would eventually enable me to solve the problem, I continued driving as if nothing was wrong.

Two weeks later, The Plan malfunctioned after our API meeting on April 11, 2015, which ended not so much on a sour note as it did not begin on a good one. Alan announced his health necessitated API being turned over to new Team Leaders. With experienced investigators Jeff and Michelle taking the reins, API would continue to be API.

As soon as I walked out of the restaurant that evening, I remembered my problem. An arrival home at dusk meant driving in the absolute dark to feed a dog belonging to my mother's friend, Jackie, who was ill. So much for The Plan. This called for The Plan 2.0.

After stopping at home, I steeled myself for the nail-biting drive to Jackie's house a mile away. Climbing behind the wheel, I turned on the ignition, eased out of our parking lot, and into The Plan 2.0. I would stop along the shoulder each time the lights disappeared, turn off the engine, and then repeatedly restart it until the headlights reappeared.

The lights did not flicker once.

Talk about lucky. Guess I better get this thing into the shop as soon as I can come up with the money.

After my next payday, the local mechanic kept the car a full day before giving up on curing the problem. I resurrected The Plan and The Plan 2.0, while asking acquaintances for referrals to repair shops. None of the mechanics I called would work on probable electrical problems.

It happened again on Wednesday, May 6. Another tense drive to feed Jackie's dog, and another trip with not so much as a blink by my headlights.

The final straw came later that month. A friend needed a ride home following an out-patient procedure at a Fayetteville hospital. I knew we should be home by dusk, but I still prepared myself for another scary road trip should her procedure take longer than expected.

We drove home with steady, bright headlights all the way.

Whew, that's three trips now. Kind of a lot for coincidences. Could Dave be...no, no. It's coincidence.

Deciding the car had a computer problem, I passed the idea on to the local mechanic and lost my car for another full day. He still could not find the culprit, so I did the unthinkable. I contacted a random auto repair shop listed in the Yellow Pages. Within 20 minutes, the problem was found and fixed.

***

Carol Martindale-Taylor

On Tuesday, June 16, four of us gathered for a lunch many weeks in the making due to conflicting schedules. Lorraine insisted I meet her friend Jan, because Jan was interested in paranormal investigating. On this particular day, Lorraine's brother completed our foursome at a restaurant in nearby Farmington.

Munching our way through one-of-a-kind sandwiches, the conversation quickly turned to ghost hunting and all things paranormal.

"My biggest concern is always whether or not I am making too much out of things that are coincidences," I said, surveying the group from over my sandwich.

"There is no such thing as a coincidence," Jan said between lady-like bites. Two heads nodded in agreement. Mine remained stationary.

"I don't know. A series of incidents with my headlights has me wondering. I'm not sure how much to write off as coincidence, and how much might have been caused by someone unseen helping me."

"I repeat, there is no such thing as coincidence."

The same heads bobbed up and down while chewing.

"Okay, see what all of you think about this," and I launched into my failing headlights story.

"So now I worry about putting too much into the idea that Dave was somehow protecting me, when it truly was a coincidence." I returned to my half-eaten sandwich.

"There is no such thing," all three said, sliding empty plates to the center of the table.

As we bounced ideas off each other, Jan stared at the brick wall over my right shoulder. I assumed she was lost in thought contemplating our deep discussion.

"Ah, Carol, he's here right now."

Lorraine neglected to tell me Jan is psychic.

"Who's what?"

"Dave. He's here now. He's right there," she said, nodding toward the vacant wall beyond my shoulder.

"Is he really here?" A shiver flowed down the entire right side of my body, the same side where I often sensed him hovering.

"Yes, and he says it was him working with your headlights."

"Oh, my God."

No bobbing heads now. All eyes tracked back and forth between Jan and the brick wall.

"As a matter of fact, he says that if you really think back, you'll remember other times when it was him too."

"Oh, my God."

"Can you tell when he's around you?"

"Sometimes I think I feel him near me."

"Where do you feel like he is whenever he's near you?"

"Over my right shoulder. He always used to sit on my right side too."

"Well, that's where he is right now."

"Oh, my God."

Jan's shoulders slumped. Her eyes shifted back to mine.

"He's gone. I repeat, there is no such thing as coincidence," she whispered in her low, knowing tone.

"Oh, my God."

LETTER TO DAVE
MAY 9 TO JULY 12, 2015

Dear Dave:

Sat., May 9, 2015. Psychics and psychic researchers think we pre-plan our lives, so why did we agree to this plan? It seems like a lot of heartbreak and pain to learn a lesson.

I made a copy of the news article on the internet about your accident. Now that I know you are okay, it is easier to read. I just hope you did not suffer, and that your soul left immediately.

Thu., May 28, 2015. My automatic headlights have been malfunctioning, and I have had three scary drives home. However, they never so much as flickered during those trips. Are you helping me?

Tue., June 16, 2015. I had lunch with a psychic today—and you! You did protect me by making those headlights work, and it looks like you have been with me for a long time.

Psychic Allyson Walsh thinks you might have been on a mission. Maybe you have.

Thu., June 18, 2015. You did it again! It felt like one finger pushed the bed sheet down against my shoulder. I suppose one day I will get to see how you do that, but right now, it is pure magic.

Sat., June 20, 2015. The more I think about what you have done, the more I realize how truly lucky I am. Not many people ever know this kind of comfort.

Tue., June 30, 2015. Looking at our pictures reminded me of how physically close we liked to get. I could swear after you left, even when having sex with someone, there was a part of me that cringed when confronted with being close to someone else.

Mon., July 6, 2015. I am pretty sure I am supposed to learn patience this time around (boy, am I messing up on that one), but why have I been on my own for so long, even when I was married? I have not accomplished anything great by staying here after you left.

I wonder what you would be doing if you were still here, or here with someone else. Oh, I do not like that thought. Terrific, now I am jealous of your spirit!

Sat., July 11, 2015. We never used the word 'love.' yet it is so obvious in our pictures that my friends comment on it. Words...they are only words. Cliff and I said "I love you" to each other every day, almost until the very day we split up.

Sun., July 12, 2015. My picture of your headstone popped up on my screen today! Were you trying to tell me you first came to me the Sunday after you died?

Love,
Carol

THE HEADSTONE

In 2015, the days of the week matched those in 1964, so on Friday, July 10, 2015, I found myself wondering when Dave first realized he died. Did he know right away, or did it take time? And if he came to me as I suspect he did, when did he do it?

Thoughts of blithely watching TV that Friday night while he lay dying on Long Beach pavement flit through my head. I imagined rubber-necking drivers hoping to catch a glimpse of his body. I remembered how Saturday morning, still in blissful ignorance, I waited for his phone call, and how by Sunday evening, I knew something was very wrong.

With all this muddling its way through my mind, I decided it was time to stop thinking about it and get busy reviewing video from our last API investigation. Watching hours of video from cameras focused on inanimate objects is the ultimate in boredom, but it is how we find some of our best paranormal evidence. We grin and bear it.

Anything more mechanical than a fork, and I am in trouble, so using a flash drive for the first time was challenging.

Where do I insert this darn thing?

When folder names accidently appeared on the screen, they made no sense, so I clicked on the first one hoping for enlightenment.

Dave's headstone!

I sank back into my chair.

Is he telling me he didn't know he was dead until this date in 1964? Or was it the day he first came to me? Or is this one of those coincidences that never happen?

My intuition said two days after the accident was when he first came to me. Intuition does not prove anything.

My picture of his headstone popping up, one incident in a growing number of such occurrences, spoke volumes about his strong personality and determination. Did he have the same capacity soon after the accident, but I missed his clues?

If only we could talk.

LETTER TO DAVE
JULY 17 TO SEPTEMBER 6, 2015

Dear Dave:

Fri., July 17, 2015. I recently thought of you as the strong, silent type much like my father. It must take tremendous determination, will power and energy to do the things you have done for me. As a young woman, I wished for the love of one great man in my lifetime. I had it all along and did not know it. I find myself wondering what I did to deserve you.

By talking to you, am I keeping you here when you should move on?

Sat., July 18, 2015. I have not felt you around me since the headstone picture came up. Was it your goodbye? I do not want to let you go now that I found you again after all these years. I am being selfish, and can only hope it does not make you angry or disappointed in me.

Sun., July 19, 2015. Where do you go when you are not here? To watch over your sister? See your mother? Make peace with your father?

Mon., Aug. 3, 2015. I wonder how I would feel if our circumstances were switched. Would it bother me to see you with Lisa or other women?

   Sat., Aug. 7, 2015. What would our kids have looked like?

   Thu., Aug. 11, 2015. Jan saw you that day over lunch. Not in your uniform, but your face. She thought we made a beautiful couple. We did...do...

   Mon., Aug. 17, 2015. I wanted to have sex with you so much, but I was not raised that way. Would I have given in before we got married? Would I have had your baby, and have part of you with me today?

   Tues., Aug. 25, 2015. You will always be a gorgeous young man while I gray, gain weight and add wrinkle after wrinkle. Oh yeah, spirits do not care about physical bodies because they are only temporary vessels—I still do not like it! Would you have chased after the 25-year-olds once we were in our 40s and 50s?

   Wed., Sept. 2, 2015. Was that you early this morning pushing down on my bed, right behind my knees?

   Sun., Sept. 6, 2015. Can you feel me when you touch me? I would love to feel you, feel your touch, skin on skin. Instead, my mattress is having all the fun!

   Tue., Sept. 8, 2015. I had lunch today with Jan, Lorraine and you. My life could not get any better than it is this very day.

   Love,
   Carol

THE GREATER GOOD

"Hey, how about getting together tomorrow? Maybe Jan can join us," I suggested.

Lorraine's telephone call prompted my idea. We had such fun digging into the unknown the last time we got together, a second round sounded inviting.

"Sure, I'll give her a call. Does 11:15 work at the same restaurant?"

"Yep. Hope you can drag her along."

My short drive the next morning provided enough time to consider the possibilities.

I hope Lorraine convinced Jan to come along. She seems like fun, and she's sure interesting to talk to. Besides, it would be great if Dave showed up again.

Turning into the parking lot, I found a space along the road where my vehicle could easily be seen, and killed the engine. Dragging out my comb and lipstick, I tipped my rear view mirror down.

Damn, another one.

I yanked out a gray hair standing at attention, waving an invitation to its buddies.

I wish there was some place to take classes about this stuff before I'm too old to learn how to do it.

Lowering my window, I watched the strand of silver sail off on a puff of air breezing past my car.

Lorraine's white 4x4 pulled in next to me, interrupting my train of thought. Exiting our cars, we met at her vehicle's rear hatch.

"Hey, good to see ya," I yelled above the traffic.

"You too. Let's go on inside. Jan shouldn't be far behind me."

Heading for the same round table used during our last visit, we unloaded handbags and walked ten feet to the counter. Studying the overhead menu, backs to the front door, Jan walked up behind us.

"Hi you two. Good to see everybody. Sorry I'm late."

"Hey there. No, you're not late. Lorraine and I just got here. We haven't even ordered."

Food painstakingly selected, we headed for our table and made small talk until someone called out our names. Carrying plates loaded with specialty sandwiches and chips, we worked our way back to the table, losing ourselves in the large living-room style chairs.

A few bites later, the small talk ended.

"Well, you really have me going with this Dave stuff. At least now I know it's not my imagination when I think he's hovering over my right shoulder. You won't believe some of the other things he's done to let me know he's around."

My tales about Dave were approaching a steady roll when Jan's right hand abandoned her sandwich. She waved at the wall behind me.

"Ah, he's here again, in the same place." She nodded at the now familiar blank wall.

I've got chills all down my right side again.

"Good grief, I've never seen this before!" Jan's voice held a sense of awe. "It's like he's living life with you. I can actually see energy passing between the two of you, and I usually see that only with someone who recently transitioned."

"That's interesting, because after I decided it really is him, I realized that out of the men I've known, he had the strongest personality. He's the one who could do this."

"He's telling me you two planned for him to leave here early, and how he did it for the greater good."

The greater good?

"I wonder if we've been together before. If we have a history."

"I think you have."

"Yeah, but as friends, or family, or lovers?"

"I say romantically."

Still thinking about us as lovers in the past, I missed someone's joke. I did not miss Jan's reaction.

"That's hilarious, even Dave's laughing!"

A sense of humor on the Other Side?

"Oh, oh. He's fading. He's gone."

She saw us again.

"You know," I said as I relaxed back into the comfort of my chair, "as a teenager, he survived a bad crash while driving drunk. He used a designated driver after that, but he still died in a car wreck. I guess it really was meant to happen."

"Yes. Yes, it was." Jan's fork traced through crumbs on her plate.

LETTER TO DAVE
SEPTEMBER 11 TO SEPTEMBER 14, 2015

Dear Dave:

Fri., Sept. 11, 2015. I can barely stand the thought of you disappearing. I am scared it is going to happen all over again. I must drive you nuts, but you love me anyway!

Mon., Sept. 14, 2015. I sent Jan an e-mail about smelling Old Spice in my room recently. The night before she read it, she was in a hotel room in Michigan getting the strong scent of Old Spice and a quick picture of you, making her wonder what I was doing at that moment.

KEEP YOUR EYES OPEN GIRL

I could not resist a direct pipeline to Dave. Two weeks after our last luncheon, Jan and I spent four hours over another meal at what was now our hangout.

"I am so glad Lorraine got us together," I said, opening the restaurant door for her.

"Me too. I've always wanted to meet ghost hunters. By the way, thanks for the invitation to your API investigation. An old TB sanatorium has to have a ton of activity in it."

"Yeah, it does. We have a home investigation in Sulphur Springs first, but the sanatorium is the biggie. Every group going there gets good video and voice recordings."

Food ordered, we nestled down at our usual table.

"By the way, someone unrelated to the TB sanatorium is going to show up during that investigation," Jan said, scooting her chair up to the table. "Someone is going to just stop in for a visit."

"That's interesting, I wonder who that could be," I called over my shoulder as I headed for the counter and my food.

With Jan right behind me picking up her order, we settled back down and started on another subject.

"Okay, so what's going on these days?" she asked, wrapping slender fingers around pita bread stuffed with grilled chicken.

"Let's see. Oh yeah, this morning. I'm in bed thinking about what I need to do today, and I feel this swipe across my left knocker. What does it mean when you're hoping it's a ghost getting a quick feel?"

The visual made us giggle.

"And yesterday, one of the senior men at the center asked me to go for a drive with him this Sunday."

"Really? Are you going?" She stopped in mid bite.

"No way. Oh, he's nice enough, but in the first place, I'm married, and in the second, I'm not interested anyway. Now that Dave said he'll be waiting for me when I cross over, I don't need a third man in my life."

Jan's head cocked sideways, reminiscent of the old RCA dog logo.

"I'm hearing 'keep your eyes open girl'."

"What?"

"I don't see him, but that's what I'm hearing."

"Well, I can't do much about it. There's no way I'd ever leave Delonte. With all his health problems, and trapped the way he is, it would kill him."

"I guess so." Jan's concentration went back to her now cold fries.

"Besides, one man on this side and one on the other are enough," I laughed.

"Ha, I see what you mean."

"Changing the subject Jan, do you know any groups in Fayetteville working to expand their abilities to tune into the universe? I know there are classes you can take, but I've never seen any advertised around here."

"I don't know of any either, but I'd like to join one. I used to work with a group in Houston."

"And speaking of things like that," I interrupted, "I got word from Mark Johnson, that hypnotist who does past life regression sessions. He's scheduling appointments in Oklahoma City, so I plan to set one up. Maybe he can help me clear my jumbled brain and open up to the Other Side."

"If he's good, he probably can."

Launching into other subjects kept us going for another two hours before I looked at my watch.

"Oops, time for me to head out of here."

"Me too. Listen, there are some books you can read to help yourself open up." Grabbing paper and pen out of my purse, I jotted down the list Jan rattled off for my reading assignments.

"Keep your eyes open girl" played over and over in my head until I walked into the local library with my reading list.

Pulling out of the library parking lot empty handed, I still laughed. How many women can say a ghost tickled their knocker?

LETTER TO DAVE
SEPTEMBER 23 TO SEPTEMBER 29, 2015

Dear Dave:

Wed., Sept. 23, 2015. Jan thinks you will show yourself to me (as did Allyson) when I least expect it. I hope I won't be so shocked I cannot revel in seeing you.

Tue., Sept. 29, 2015. I am watching my mother, elderly friends and the seniors at work. Can I please, please join you before I become a depressed, invalid old woman?

By the way, API has an investigation coming up in Sulphur Springs. You are welcome to join us.

Love,
Carol

THAT FIRST INVESTIGATION

The first Saturday in October was a chilly day. Driving into the small town of Sulphur Springs, we threw on our jackets as we parked in the client's driveway.

Piling out of the car, the four of us headed to the front door where a 30-something bearded man stood holding the door open.

"Hi, I'm Bill."

"Hi Bill. I'm Jeff, this is my wife Michelle, her son Christian, and Carol, one of our Lead Investigators."

"Good to meet all of you. Come on in, and please excuse the condition of the house. We bought it from our landlord last month, so I've started ripping out drywall and electrical wiring. Please be careful. I don't want anyone getting electrocuted!"

"Don't worry, we're used to working around things in the dark. Besides, doing renovations can help stir things up, so maybe we'll get some good evidence."

Closing the door behind us, our client ushered us into a barren living room where we listened to tales of lights turning off and on by themselves, and a shadow person seen several times by their six-year-old son. He often saw it walk across the dining room, and then disappear through floor boards in the adjoining utility room.

After setting up cameras in the active areas, we began the investigation with our opening prayer of protection—although not religious, I take protection whenever I can.

Boredom set in as we tracked an assortment of orbs bouncing around rooms, but not much else. The most activity in the early evening happened when a K-2 electromagnetic meter spiked over a collection of dusty crystals displayed on a built-in living room shelf.

"Okay, let's try the SB-7. Maybe we can get something with it." Jeff lifted the gadget out of his black bag of tricks.

He and I walked into the dining room while Michelle followed us with a night vision camera rolling. Setting up along the opposite wall, she filmed us as we took seats around a dining room table and faced her son who was wrapping up a voice recording session.

"Get ready for a headache," I muttered in his direction. The grating static coming from an SB-7 metal canister makes some tear up, but in theory, it enables spirits to use its rapid radio waves to create words.

"Okay, this contraption won't hurt you, and maybe you can use it to make words and talk to us." Jeff held the device at chest level, extending the attached microphone toward the center of the table.

"Is there anyone here with us?" His question drew no immediate response at first, but finally the box crackled alive.

"Dave" came through the static.

"Hello, Dave. Is there anyone else here with you?"

The box spewed out "Jeff."

"Yes, that's me. Now we don't want to chase anyone away, but the owners would like to know who is here. Are you the shadow person who walks across the living room and disappears into the utility room?"

Nothing.

"Their little boy sees whoever it is, and it scares him. Is that what you want to do?"

Still nothing.

Holding his palm over the box's speaker to muffle the racket, he looked at us.

"Let's be quiet and listen for a while to see if anything happens without prompting it."

Silent minutes ticked away.

"Okay, that does it. Let's switch to the Ovulis." Jeff shut down the SB-7, made a quick trip to his magician's bag, and returned with the Ovulis.

Setting the transistor radio-sized box on the table in front of him, he flipped it on.

"Now this does not make noise, but it might be easier for you to use. Please come close so it can pick up the information it needs."

"Paranormal," the Ovulis called out in its mechanical voice. Its LCD screen confirmed what we heard.

"Yes, paranormal. That's why we are here. What about the paranormal?"

"Carol," the Ovulis said, confirming my name in print.

It said my name!

After no further communication, we packed up for the night, and closed the investigation with our prayer telling entities they cannot go home with us.

Half awake as we pulled out of the client's driveway, I closed my eyes.

Dave, paranormal, then Carol. Seven years of ghost hunting and the spirits suddenly know my name?

I dozed off against a hopefully locked door.

LETTER TO DAVE
OCTOBER 17 TO NOVEMBER 1, 2015

Dear Dave:

Sat., Oct. 17, 2015. I got home at 4:35 a.m. this morning, after our big ghost hunt in the old Booneville TB sanatorium. The whole session was recorded, so we'll see what the evidence shows.

Mon., Oct. 19, 2015. I understand your pictures do not show the spirit you, but you had damn good taste when you picked out that body!

Sun., Nov. 1, 2015. I felt that; my blanket was pushed against the middle of my back, and I knew it was you. It made me smile.
Delonte called tonight. He is having a rough time mentally. He needs a new TV, but since his family is starting to visit, and Mom and I will both send him money for Christmas anyway, I am not going to pay for it. I guess I am getting selfish, but I feel different knowing why I let him into my life.

Love,
Carol

WHO ARE YOU?

An October day in Arkansas can be anything. This one, in the middle of the month, rated up there with the best of the best. Cruising south down I-49 from Fayetteville, miles of high, hilly greenery passed with ease. I soaked in the sunny view knowing the return trip would be made while forcing myself to stay awake.

The choice parking spots at the massive old TB sanatorium were filling up with API folks by the time I arrived. Investigations at such hot spots draw people who normally pass on our residential cases, so I was not surprised by the number of cars.

Not my first investigation there, I already knew the lay of the land. The first floor is used by the state government as the administration center for a campus serving state mental health patients. Its typical hospital-style hallways with rooms jutting off both sides are in stark contrast to the floors above and below them.

Ceilings in the upper floors of the football-field long building are collapsing onto the floors beneath them. Curls of lead paint decorate walls, and unlit stairwells are cluttered with crumbling bricks cascading down their side walls.

In fact, given the condition of the site, it is feared that in the near future, access will no longer be granted for paranormal investigations. Those with hypersensitivity to such contaminates as mold and dust are already on the fringe of unsafe conditions.

Even though a repeat visit for me, when I joined other investigators gathering outside the back entrance, I was just as anxious to get started as those investigating the sanatorium for the first time.

"Okay, for those of you who have never been here before, be careful, and never, ever work alone," Jeff announced. "Watch your step in the stairwells, and when walking the hallways, always remember there are cooling units hanging low from the ceilings. If you're over five feet tall, you will get a concussion. Be aware of areas where there are molds on the walls and peeling lead paint. If anyone wants them, we have paper face masks available. Also, know that during our last investigation, we found pigeons in rooms on the fourth floor. Any questions?"

Ghosts okay, but I won't be going on the fourth floor again.

He waited through our momentary silence.

"Okay, let's haul the gear inside and put it in the conference room on the first floor. We'll work out of there, and set up our command center outside that door. Load up and follow me."

Anticipation out-running us, bodies scattered around vehicles to grab cameras, tripods and computer equipment for the command center tables. Cases stuffed with small electronics, grocery bags of munchies and personal equipment items were hauled inside and parked on the interior conference room table.

Then our work really began.

Two hours later, extension cords dangled through stairwells, connecting cameras on the second, third and fourth floors to our command center on the first. With everything in place, we headed for the nearest stairway going up.

The second floor upsets even returning paranormal investigators. The aluminum Christmas tree, long since losing its luster to airborne dust, and trimmed with dingy colored ornaments, stops them in their tracks. But even that does not make the lump in their throats. That happens when they see the rusted, tiny red tricycle parked alongside it. They realize they are in the children's ward.

Old hospital records show children coming in not only as patients, but as healthy youngsters relegated to staying with sick parents. A few babies were born here as well, but how many ever saw the outside world is unknown.

The third floor appears normal until you notice the thick plexiglass doors at one end, chopping the floor into separate units. It is what it looks like; a way to separate certain patients from others. 'The Cage' housed patients who were either violent, or convicted of violent crimes.

Because of all the horrors no doubt perpetrated there, paranormal investigators are drawn to The Cage. Its four empty rooms, dusty and stale smelling, never fail to make them hopeful, and they are seldom disappointed.

Once stationed around this quarantine area, we began our investigation. K-2 meters raced from green to red, and words crackled through the SB-7 spirit box, including Alan's name being called out three times.

Then the SB-7 uttered specific instructions. Intrigued when told to go to the basement for something special, everyone headed for the nearest exit.

Leading the group down dark stairwells, I gingerly stepped over jumbled wall tiles spilling out on landings between floors, until we arrived back on the first floor.

Jan, watching the video cameras in the command center, called out as I exited the doorway.

"Carol, there was someone walking right in front of you as you came down the stairs."

"Well, it sure wasn't a living person. There was no one in front of me all the way down."

"I know, but I saw a shadow person right smack ahead of you on those last few steps."

After the last investigator spilled out of the exit, we congregated around the command center tables.

"Okay, we've been told to go to the basement, so go we will," Jeff announced for the benefit of those who had not been on the third floor with us. "Everyone stick together, and use your flashlights or your camera's LCD screen for lighting. Watch for things stacked against the walls and on the floor down there. We'll head for the old cafeteria and set up there for a spirit box session."

Falling in behind him, he led us through the basement stairwell. Exiting at the bottom, a sharp left took us down a blackened hallway smelling of damp cement and moldy cardboard boxes.

No wonder they had a Halloween fund-raising event down here last year, I thought as my flashlight revealed fake spider webs spun across the entrance to a very real morgue.

Flashlights and LCD screens illuminated pin-point floor areas around our feet as we entered the cavernous former cafeteria. Milling around in the dark, we each picked out a vantage point along the walls, while Jeff and Jan retrieved folding chairs from those leaning on the wall behind them. Wiping them off, they sat down near the center of the room, and Michelle snapped on the night vision camera.

"Okay, we were told on the third floor to come down here for something special. So here we are." With the squawking box held steady in front of him, Jeff scanned the darkness.

"Carol, is there someone behind you?" Jan called out over the infernal screeching.

"Yes," the box loudly responded.

Laughter broke out when Beckie, one of our other Lead Investigators, stepped out of the shadows behind me.

"Okay. Now can you do something," Jeff asked, "anything to let us know you're here? Can you move something?"

"Yes," the box answered.

"Good. Then please do so. Do something to let us know you are here."

Collective breaths were held for several seconds before the SB-7 came back to life.

"Carol," squawked the box.

"Yes, Carol is here. So is Alan, Jesse, Mike… Who are you?"

"Dave."

"Did you work here?" asked Jan.
"No."
"Okay, then were you a patient here?"
"No."
I had no trouble staying awake on my long drive home.

LETTER TO DAVE
NOVEMBER 21 TO DECEMBER 26, 2015

Dear Dave:

Sat., Nov. 21, 2015. You were in Oklahoma City for my past life regression yesterday! Amelia, the Gypsy woman I saw as myself, and her husband Isahkoff (you) made sense, but what about Jimmy, the British soldier? How could his life overlap with my current life?

I am sending in my DNA for analysis. It should be almost all Eastern European; do I have a physical connection with Amelia?

Tue., Nov. 24, 2015. I replaced the headlight you burned out on my way to Oklahoma City, and laughed all the way to the repair shop!

Mon., Dec. 7, 2015. I am seeing so many TV commercials about young couples picking out engagement rings for Christmas. That is something I never had, but why does it bother me now?

Sat., Dec. 26, 2015. I found a theory that spirits can split into concurrent lives, each keeping the essence of the whole. One part even remains in the spirit world. That might explain soldier Jimmy co-existing with me.

Carol Martindale-Taylor

    Love,
    Carol

PAST LIVES

The I-40 West road sign reflecting an early morning sun temporarily blinded me, but it posed no problem. After years of driving this route, I knew each hill and bend in the road by heart. Without touching the steering wheel again, driving 700 miles due west would put me cruising down Central Avenue into the heart of Albuquerque.

Many, many times I considered leaving Arkansas and Maryland behind me. It never happened, and it would not this time either. I would be in Oklahoma City this one night, and return to Prairie Grove the next morning.

It was Friday, November 20, 2015, and Mark Johnson, a hypnotherapist from the Newton Center in Texas, scheduled me for a hypnosis session at 2:00 that afternoon. Rather than experience only a past life regression, I opted for the additional Quantum Healing session. It would include efforts to bring my spirit guides forward, and to heal any lingering issues from previous life times.

Questions, so many questions. Johnson needed a list of them to help direct our session, but there were many I asked only myself.

Could he put me under? Probably. In San Diego, I participated in a group session where I successfully went under, so I knew about time warping, and the wondrous things the mind can do. During that session, I developed an itch. My thinking went something like, I have an itch. It's only an itch. It'll go away. No need to scratch it.

Will this session bring past lives to the surface? Which ones? Was I a Gypsy as intuition tells me? Why do I feel so at home in Newfoundland? Why do I have so much empathy for minorities? Will I meet my guides, and more than anything else, will Dave be there?

Jan assured me Dave will never quit me. As she put it, "It is written in stone. He will always be here, now and into infinity. He is so waiting for you." Will this session confirm her insight about our relationship?

And so the Interstate miles passed as I soaked up the warmth of a sun filtering through my back window. Admiring herds of coal black cattle grazing on the last greenery of fall, I watched small town America slip in and out of view.

Oh, oh! What was that?

A tingle passed through me, then a sheet of rough goose bumps broke the surface down the length of my right arm. I checked the dashboard clock.

It's 9:20. Okay Dave, if that was you, thanks for riding shotgun with me. I know I'm going to need help finding my motel in the dark tonight.

A few wrong turns later, I found the holistic health center Johnson uses when he visits from Texas. Arriving early, I ate at a neighborhood diner and killed time contemplating the universe from my own planet.

Is Dave really, truly with me now? Will he be with me when I'm under hypnosis?

One mediocre meal down, I circled back to the center and parked along the side of the building. My headlights stopped short of brushing the tall, manicured hedge shielding office windows from intense sunsets.

Within minutes of sitting down in the lobby, a man approached me

"Hi Carol, I'm Mark Johnson. Sorry to keep you waiting. Come on in, and make yourself comfortable."

Is that voice natural? No wonder he can hypnotize people.

He motioned me through the door and into a comfortable black recliner near an over-sized mahogany desk. Sinking his large frame into a chair between the desk and my feet, he stationed his voice recorder within reaching distance before focusing on me.

After discussions about my life as it is today, and comparing notes about the paranormal—he is a 'sensitive' and his wife helps spirits cross over—we settled into the business of putting my mind elsewhere.

Setting up my own recording equipment as he started his, he then began putting me under hypnosis by talking me into a calm, open frame of mind.

No easy task.

Guiding me through breathing exercises, he next had me close my eyes.

"Okay, now let yourself relax. Starting at the very top of your head, feel the muscles become loose and limp. Loose and limp. Let them release starting at the top of your head, becoming loose and limp as they work their way down your face, down your neck. Feel your shoulders soften, relax, sag under their own weight."

Once my body relaxed, next came my racing mind.

"Imagine yourself walking down, down, down a stairway. You are going deeper and deeper into a calm, comfortable place. You are relaxed. Your mind is clear. You feel so good. You are moving deeper and deeper down. Each time you hear the words blue rose, you go even deeper, deeper down. Deep into a peaceful place. Blue rose, blue rose."

Am I under? I don't feel under. He said I would feel this way, so maybe I am under.

"Okay, now take me to a fun time when you were ten years old. You are ten years old and having fun. What is going on? What are you doing? Tell me what you see."

"My pony. It's my tenth birthday party, and my Dad is taking my friends for rides on my pony. He's walking each of them around the yard."

That scene fully explored, Mark asked me to go back to an earlier time.

"Okay, now you are in your mother's womb. What is it like in the womb? How do you feel?"

"It's warm and dark. I don't like it. I feel like I'm in the wrong place. I don't belong there."

"So you don't belong there. What do you do about it?"

"I go back."

"Back where?"

"Back to my spirit friends."

"Okay, so what happens there?"

"We talk it over. They tell me I really need to return."

"How old are you when this happens?"

"Four months."

"So what did you do?"

"I returned to the womb."

"Were you unhappy about doing that?"

"No, not really. Just resigned."

"How old were you when you returned to the womb?"

"Seven months. I was seven months old."

Did I really experience this? It might explain some things.

Mark next prepared me to move back to a previous life.

"Now you are further back in time. You are in the last life time before this one. Where are you? What do you see? Describe it to me."

"A campfire. I see a campfire. We're all standing around it, talking about leaving. My husband is the leader of our band, and we're worried because the local townspeople are coming to chase us out."

"Why would people chase you away?"

"Gypsies. Dirty Gypsies. Nobody wants us around. We're thieves. We have to keep moving."

Is this real, or my imagination? Has my intuition been right all along, or did I create this scene?

"Isahkoff. My husband's name is Isahkoff. I am called Amelia."

"If he's the leader or head man of your group, does that mean you are something special like a queen of the Gypsies?"

"No, not really. I'm just his wife."

We went through this life until Isahkoff and his horse were killed in an accident, and Amelia died at a young age from pneumonia.

"Tell me, did you recognize Isahkoff as someone in this life?"

"Yes, yes. He was Dave."

"So you two have been together before?"

"Yes, I have been with him in all my lifetimes, in some form or other. We'll be together again in another life."

"Is there a social agreement between the two of you then? Is that why he left here early?"

"Yes, but he helps me from the Other Side. He has not reincarnated."

"Let's talk about when he left this life. You said you did not know for four months what happened to him. Did he plan that?"

"Yes."

"Okay. Now you were concerned about when his soul left his body. What can you tell me about that?"

"During the accident. He left during the accident."

"You were also wondering when he first came to you after the accident. Can you tell me about that?"

"He came to me the Sunday after the accident."

"What else does Dave do?"

"I am learning to let my husband go, and Dave is working with me on that."

"Does Dave have a message for you?"

"I'll always be with you."

"Good. That's good. Now let's move on to your life just before this one, before you were a Gypsy. What do you see now?"

"Open fields all around me. I am walking down a dirt road. I see long, low rock walls dividing up pastures."

"What are you doing? Where are you going?"

"I'm walking home when I am not supposed to be doing that."

"Why is that?"

"It's 1940 in Great Britain, and I am stationed with soldiers in a small camp along the coast near my home. I'm going AWOL."

"What does your family think about that?"

"My mother and two younger sisters are glad to see me, but my father is upset."

After guiding me through the life of 19-year-old Jimmy who went on to survive the war and die an old man, Mark asked me about prior lives. Although sensing my drowning death as a fisherman off Newfoundland, and life as a Native American in the Southwest, I felt it was not necessary to explore those lives.

Am I creating these lives because I expect them?

"Okay. Now you mentioned dying of pneumonia when you were Amelia. I recall that during our conversation before you left the present, you talked about not being able to draw deep breaths. Even a doctor mentioned this to you. This may be related to Amelia's death from a breathing problem."

He stopped, as if listening to something.

"Yes, yes. She is apologizing. She did not mean to pass that on to you. She can take it away from you right now. Do you want her to do that?"

Oh yeah, he's a sensitive. He can pick up on things.

"Yes, please."

A few seconds pass in quiet.

"It's done. Very soon you should feel relief from this problem."

We'll see. I'll draw a deep breath now, and...that came from deep down inside me! Did she really do that, or was it the power of suggestion?

"Now I want you to go deeper and deeper down. Blue rose, blue rose. Think about blue rose as you sink deeper and deeper down. Your mind is calm and clear, calm and clear when you arrive deep, deep down. Your guides will meet you there. Tell me who is with you."

"Thomas. He says his name is Thomas."

"Okay, hello Thomas. Now Thomas, what can you tell us about Carol. Does she receive messages from the Other Side, and if she does, can you tell us how she receives them? Does she hear them? See them?"

"What she receives is done through intuition. She senses things."

Whoa, where did my deeper voice come from?

"If Carol wants to meet with you, can she seek you out for help?"

"Yes, I will meet with her."

"Okay Carol, whenever you want to meet with Thomas for guidance, use blue rose to put yourself under. Pick any place you like, some special place, and ask him to meet you there."

Mark stopped talking and listened again.

"Now, wait a minute…I'm getting the feeling Dave is here. Yes, he's almost forcing me to say he'll be there too. He'll come too."

You're here!

Soon after that, Mark brought me back to the present.

With instructions on how to put myself under in a place of peace and openness, he gave me the tools needed to meet with Thomas—or hang out with Dave. In addition to the time spent talking with Mark, I was actually under hypnosis for four and a half solid hours.

Surprisingly limber after sitting in the same position all that time, I headed out the door and into the night. Finding my car, I started the engine and stared into that tall hedge. My driver's side headlight was missing in action.

An instant of dread, then laughter.

I knew it! That's what happened this morning. You needed energy from somewhere didn't you? Well, it's okay babe, I can deal with it. Now let's get me to my motel room, and then find someplace to eat at this hour of the night.

LETTER TO DAVE
JANUARY 3 TO APRIL 17, 2016

Dear Dave:

Sun., Jan. 3, 2016. Jan thinks I am close to physically seeing energy, and my guide Thomas said I was intuitive. I do get feelings about people, so maybe the ability is there, but dormant.

Sat., Jan. 23, 2016. I met two people this week who need help. They may be having psychic experiences, but are being treated for schizophrenia. They both died, but were brought back to life—one several times. What is happening to them does not sound like mental illness (okay, so I am not a doctor). Maybe I at least gave them hope since they both think they are going crazy.

Thu., Jan. 28, 2016. In a vision yesterday, Michelle saw a man leaning against a tree like he was waiting for someone. There was no message, but she knew the vision was for me.

Thu., Feb. 4, 2016. My DNA results arrived, and I am 1/3 British Isles. What about Michelle's vision of a man waiting in a place that looks like the British Isles?

Wed., Feb. 10, 2016. While practicing clearing my head this

morning, I saw the blurry flash of a sailor from waist high, in dress whites, and with arms folded as though resting on a table. No features, but the right build for you.

By the way, after thinking it over for the last few years, I have decided to move to Costa Rica after I retire. It will be my second-to-last big adventure. We know what the last will be.

Sun., Mar. 6, 2016. I do not know if I was secure enough to ignore women making passes at you. Maybe it would have been rough for us, but smoothed out when you lost your hair and grew a pot belly!

Tue., Mar. 8, 2016. Poor Delonte. He turned 57 yesterday, and ended up in tears on the phone last night. He talked about how he could not have made it this far without me. I still wonder about giving him false hope, and if it is the right thing to do.

Fri., Apr. 1, 2016. As a young girl, I wanted children, but by the time I married Cliff, I did not. Did I become afraid of strong attachments after you died?

Sun., Apr. 17, 2016. Delonte called this morning for my birthday (early because he expects the prison to go into lockdown). A new case manager is interested in him, so hopefully he can get into medium security and start working on parole...but I cannot imagine being in bed with him or any other man now.

Love,
Carol

VISION VS. DNA

I noticed the e-mail before heading off to work on a wintery morning. Pre-heating my icy car had to wait.

"I just had a vision," Michelle's message began, "and it was connected to you. I saw a man leaning against a tree like he was waiting for someone. I didn't see features because it was dark, like the sun was just coming up. The tree was in a field with a low fog on the ground. He had some kind of hat on like an Irish driving cap (flat cap). Don't know what it means, and there was no message with it, but I could tell it was meant for you."

If it was for me, it could only be one man, but why somewhere that looks like England or Ireland?

I could hardly wait to get home that evening and settle down in front of my computer.

Okay, I know those caps because Grandpa used to wear them. I need to find out where they originated.

I quickly discovered the caps are from the British Isles, but there were more questions to research.

Hum, the Alligood family has a crest in merry old England, and I see 66 of them listed in local phonebooks, many with different ethnic given names. I wonder if this is all related to Michelle's vision?

I need to look at the Berhar name again.

Interested in genealogy—something we old folks often tackle before it is too late—I had already learned that Bihar and Bihari are the Gypsy/Rom spellings of Berhar, and had researched all three names.

Yep, the British white pages had 33 variations of Berhar listed, nine of which look like the same people listed under the different spellings. Some had different ethnic given names.

It was a surprising revelation given that my father's family came to the United States from Hungary. We also knew my mother's Solin family came here from Slovakia, and since the name shows up in Mexico in 1604, I suspected some might come from Spain.

Climbing into bed in the wee hours of the morning, I practiced clearing my mind, but it was open combat on foreign soil. As usual, after spending three-quarters of a century doing the opposite, I am my own worst enemy.

But I want to meet Thomas and Dave under that tree.

***

Thursday, February 4, was another freezing morning, so I bundled up before braving a head-on wind.

"Hey, Mom, I'm going to the mailbox. I'll be right back."

Walking back while sorting through a handful of mail, I opened our front door, letting a gust of icy wind cut through the living room.

"Oops, here's something from Ancestry.com. I'll bet my DNA results are ready."

Remembering the door, I slammed it behind me, and ripped the envelope open as I hustled to my bedroom. Following instructions, I accessed my Ancestry files on the internet.

"What the... Hey," I yelled out, "according to this, I'm only 56% Eastern European. I am 26% English and 6% Irish, with some minor stuff from the Iberian Peninsula and Caucus Mountains. I'm one third British Isles."

"You're what?" my mother asked as she walked in from the kitchen, wiping her hands on a dishtowel.

She peered over my shoulder while I clicked on various links and explored my results.

"How can this be? No one on either side of the family came from there," I muttered as we studied a map with colored circles delineating specific areas.

"I have no idea," she said, plopping down on my bed. "Your whole family came here from Hungary and Slovakia."

"I know, and the only reason I suspected any Iberian connection was because your family name shows up in Mexico in 1604."

After the shock wore off, she returned to her kitchen stove, and my analytical brain kicked in full force.

I've got to convince her to have her DNA studied.

It took months of cajoling and begging, but we finally submitted her sample for analysis.

Several weeks later, we received a notice that her results were ready. With both of us hovering over my computer, I pulled them up.

"Look. Only 6% from the British Isles. You're 84% Eastern European, with a minor amount from the Iberian Peninsula."

"Well, at least mine makes sense," she laughed.

I need to find that damn tree.

LETTER TO DAVE
APRIL 20 TO MAY 9, 2016

Dear Dave:

Wed., Apr. 20, 2016. My birthday today, and you did it again! How did you make your name pop up on my computer?

Tue., Apr. 26, 2016. Was that you last night—a wispy, cob web feel spreading down my face?

Mon., May 9, 2016. Delonte called yesterday. He is having a rough time with depression. The way he talked, if something happened to me or I left him, he would commit suicide. No pressure there.

Love,
Carol

A BIRTHDAY GIFT

So what if it's my birthday? I've gotta get busy. The API team's going to need this stuff soon.

After cranking up my computer, I walked to the kitchen for an uneventful tour of the refrigerator while waiting on a request for my password. Arriving back in my bedroom empty handed, I settled down for a long, hungry session.

Let's see, I'll start with Google. Maybe the client's been in the news, or is on Facebook. What was that client's name?

Fishing through my API manila file folder, I found the printed copy of their application for an investigation. There they were, the name and address, plus a list of possible paranormal activities the family is experiencing.

Thirty minutes of hunting and clicking later, nothing.

Okay, maybe I can get into their property records. Hopefully, there's more there than just their name. Let's see, oh yeah, that town's in Crawford County.

Five more minutes produced a county website with potential.

Clicking on it, a box opened requesting the property's street address. I typed it in, and my click produced a drop-down box showing three last names.

Martindale
Jones
Alligood

Alligood! And it's highlighted!

"How do you do this stuff? And thanks for my birthday gift!"

LETTER TO DAVE
MAY 23 TO MAY 26, 2016

Dear Dave:

Mon., May 23, 2016. I am sure some of the activity at the Prairie Grove Battlefield during our API investigation was you. Whenever we go on an investigation now, the Team Leaders ask me if you have been invited.

I am doctoring Chovie, the neighborhood cat, and may have to put her to sleep if a sore in her mouth does not heal. Have you been with me when I dealt with such soul-searching decisions?

Tue., May 24, 2016. Did you catch that? The good cry I had over today being the 53rd anniversary of our meeting. I guess I have to put up with this ever-lasting pain, otherwise it would mean having never met you. I cannot imagine my life without you today.

Thu., May 26, 2016. A favorite senior woman was killed in a car crash yesterday, and two other women drove to the scene to see where it happened. It made me think about people driving by while you died.

Love,
Carol

THE BATTLEFIELD INVESTIGATION

Prairie Grove Civil War Battlefield Park has a playground for children, picnic tables and buildings available to rent for private functions. Still, it is not a fun place in the usual sense of the word.

The December 7, 1862, battle witnessed the loss of 2,500 lives, the destruction of local homes and the decimation of the northern border of Arkansas. Today, this 800-acre park is quiet and serene.

Visitors can opt for a walking tour, a six-mile driving tour, or the assistance of a park interpreter for a personal tour. The grounds include a house rebuilt on its original foundation shortly after the Civil War, and buildings moved into the park recreating a period village with a church, school house, blacksmith's shop and pioneer family's homestead.

Another house, one taken over by Union military officers for staging the battle, is set up near the museum. After the Confederates retreated during the night, officers met in the house once again to make a heavy decision. They had to name the battle.

Now, as with other Civil War battlefields, the park has a reputation for being haunted, and every paranormal group investigating it has recorded activity.

Given its proximity to many of our homes, API investigated

it several times. In fact, a few years earlier while conducting a voice recording session, I asked for a name and recorded a young male voice clearly answering "Dave." I assumed he was likely a drummer boy for one side or the other, but I now question that analysis.

For our investigation on this particular night in May, we checked in with museum staff at 4:30 p.m., and then hauled our gear to the 'dog-trot' house. A popular style of home in the 1860s, its distinctive feature is an open walkway dividing the living quarters into two separate sections.

We set up our command center tables outside, facing the southern wall of the house, and stationed a camera inside that end of the structure.

Some investigators began an EVP (electronic voice phenomena) session inside, hoping to record voices not heard with their own ears, while the rest of us remained outside. We gathered around the monitor where I somehow ended up sitting squarely in front of the screen.

The cursor floated across the screen, causing a random on-screen command to pop up.

"Ah, Carol, are you playing with the mouse?" an investigator asked, leaning forward to catch my attention.

I glanced at my right hand.

"Nope. I must have brushed up against it." I moved my hand away from the gadget.

The cursor marched across the monitor again, and another uninvited command popped up.

"Okay, now I know I didn't touch it that time."

I studied the mouse, as did other investigators from their chairs near me. The red light peeking out from under it flashed on its own for nearly ten minutes before it came to a standstill.

"Well, it looks like it's finally done. I'm heading inside," I called out to those hovering over the computer. Two of us walked toward the house.

That was weird. Man, this place is active.

Softening my steps on the weathered, wooden floor of the

dog-trot breezeway, I eased through the open door in the southern half of the house.

The rest of our team stood along the walls, with Jeff positioned near an Ovulis propped up on the fireplace mantel. Gathering data from the atmosphere, the electronic box was spewing out words.

Waiting for my eyes to adjust to the minimal lighting, I leaned against the inner door frame, extending my voice recorder out in front of me. The other investigator stayed along the wall on the opposite side of the door.

New to the session, I followed our unofficial protocol, and introduced myself to whatever entities might be present.

"Hi, I just walked in. My name is Carol."

"Wave," the Ovulis called out, printing the word on its screen.

"Carol," the box called out next.

"That's a 'hi Carol'" laughed an investigator.

"Paranormal," the Ovulis said.

In all my years as an investigator, during a time in which API averaged one investigation a month, my name had never been called out. Now it had been called out for a third, and possibly an unrecorded fourth time in a row. On two of those occasions, "Dave" and "paranormal" were called out.

Why not Jim, Bob, or Charles? Why not Shirley, Ann, or Jane?

LETTER TO DAVE
JUNE 11 TO JULY 21, 2016

Dear Dave:

Sat., June 11, 2016. We looked so innocent in our pictures, yet you looked so sexy at the same time. I wish I looked sexier for you back then.

Mon., June 27, 2016. How did you put that API video between pictures of us on my computer this morning?

I had a horrible dream about you. Is that what you would have looked like if you had survived the crash? I hope there was a reason for seeing you that way because it will be in my head forever.

Sat., July 2, 2016. There it is again, 11:11 on my clock, something I have seen for decades. Will you be able to explain what repeatedly seeing it means? I read about it on the internet, and it is happening to certain people around the world, but no one knows what it means.

Sun., July 10, 2016. Thank you for the hint of Old Spice in bed this morning. Happy birthday!

Can you take the neighborhood cat with you? Maybe she could join my other four-legged friends in your realm.

Thu., July 21, 2016. You greeting me when I cross over will be the most special thing to happen in my life, but what will it mean for you? "Well, it's about damn time," or something special?

Chovie, the neighborhood cat, got a reprieve by the vet!

Love,
Carol

A MOVING TARGET

Dragging my legs out from under the sheet, I lowered my feet to the floor, tapping my toes around for an errant pair of slippers. Wiggling my way into them, I trudged into the bathroom for my morning ritual.

Finished there, it was back to my bedroom for the jeans and T-shirt I zeroed in on last night, and off to the kitchen for a glass of milk. Standing over the sink, I mentally updated my day's calendar.

Let's see. Oh yeah, it's Monday, June 27th. As soon as I get into the center, I need to work on July's operating budget.

I rinsed the glass out and went back in my bedroom.

Starting my computer, I plunked down in my re-purposed dining room chair and clicked on the e-mail icon.

Good grief, look at all that junk mail. Well, I've got some time. I'll unsubscribe from some of them right now.

I neglected checking a clock until a nagging feeling said I should.

Oops, I better feed Chovie.

As I had done for the last two years, I opened my file of Dave's pictures, and set it on the slide show function. Then I headed to the pantry for cat food.

Filling a ceramic bowl with dry food, I balanced it in one hand and opened the front door with the other. Laughing as I watched Chovie lope across the parking lot as soon as she heard the door open, I sat the food on our marble patio table. She deftly jumped straight up from the ground to the table top.

A lover and not a fighter, I sat in the plastic chair next to her while she ate so other neighborhood cats could not scare her away. Finished eating, I took her bowl inside.

After washing my hands, I headed back to my bedroom for a last minute check of e-mails before shutting the system down.

Oh, no!

A loud scratchy racket assailed me as I pushed my bedroom door open, fully anticipating a computer in its death throes.

"Yes, Carol is here. So is Alan, Jesse, Mike... Who are you?"

"Dave."

It was the API spirit box session we recorded in the TB sanatorium months earlier.

How in the world did that happen?

Looking through thumbnails of the photo album file, I found a copy of the API video lodged between the picture of Dave looking up at me from his chair during our dinner party, and the one of us in front of Mission de Alcala.

And today's the 52nd anniversary of when we talked about getting married. How do you do these things babe?

LETTER TO DAVE
JULY 30 TO SEPTEMBER 25, 2016

Dear Dave:

Sat., July 30, 2016. When a friend of my mother asked what you have done lately, I filled her in on the latest, and she commented "what he does must make me feel so very loved." You do.

Sat., Aug. 6, 2016. Delonte called. He got into an altercation with another inmate and is in administrative segregation. This could mess up his chance of getting into medium security.

Mon., Aug. 15, 2016. While working on clearing my whirling head, I had a vision of sorts. I was sailing through the air in a horizontal position; it was comfortable, with no pain and no crash landing. Did you show me your spirit leaving after being thrown out of the roadster?

Fri., Aug. 19, 2016. Something made me think about your body, and how I wish I could have made real love to it. To kiss you all over. To feel you all over. You would have needed to teach me about sex, but with your patience, I am sure we would have been good together. Later, I knew things instinctively, but I wish I had done those things for you.

Sat., Aug. 27, 2016. Delonte will not make it to Family Day this year because of the altercation with that inmate, and it messed up his chance to go into a medium security prison for another year.

I wonder what he would think about you? Well, there is no point in hurting him.

Thu., Sept. 22, 2016. I felt that brush against my right thigh last night.

Sun., Sept. 25, 2016. What did you think about my reaction at a birthday party today? A man was attracted to me and I loved the attention. With you and Delonte in my life, I would never act on anything, but it was a feeling I have not experienced for many years.

Love,
Carol

WHERE ARE THEY?

Well, *what did I do with them?*
After my eye exam, I bought new no-line bifocals, but kept my old pair for emergencies. Vain creature that I am however, I wear contact lenses while out and about, and keep old glasses handy as a level of security for driving. If my contacts became unusable, I could be stranded somewhere because I cannot drive without glasses.

Stuffing the old pair of glasses into an even older case, they landed on the floor behind the driver's seat in my car. For the summer, they kept company with an umbrella and fire extinguisher, necessities when traveling in an old car.

With fall setting in, it dawned on me to retrieve the glasses for storage in a warmer place.

"Hey, I'm going out to the car for a minute. I want to bring my old glasses inside, and I left them on the back floorboard." I almost made it to the front door.

"Throw a jacket on, it's getting cold out there," my mother warned.

"I'll only be a minute." Pretending not to hear her follow-up comment, I walked out into unusually frigid air.

Ten minutes later, fingers and nose iridescent, I walked back into the living room.

"Well, I can't find them. I looked under both front seats in case they slid under there from the back floor, and even rummaged through the glove box. Nothing."

"Well, they're around somewhere. They'll show up."

Two days passed. I dug through my car and glove box a second time, and even the trunk. No sign of the old glasses.

The day after that, I attacked my bedroom—literally. Drawers tugged open, clothes yanked out and scattered around, and then crammed back where they belong.

I gave up.

It was time for my writers' meeting by then, and I looked forward to the long drive. It was my one night a month to openly talk to Dave.

Well, it's a beautiful afternoon, and when I drive home tonight, it'll feel like Dave's with me.

Heading into Fayetteville and picking up Interstate 49 North took me toward Rogers. Settling back in my seat, I enjoyed the luxury of a light flow of traffic on an unseasonably warm day.

Man, I wish I could find those glasses. If I have trouble with my contacts tonight, I can't even drive home.

"I hate asking you for favors Dave, but I sure could use some help finding those things." The request came out of my mouth before thinking about it.

Blinking red lights ahead warned of traffic backing up, so after several minutes of stop-and-go, I pulled off the highway when I saw a familiar sign.

Ah, there's that McDonald's. I'll stop for a hamburger and set up my laptop. Maybe I can get some writing done before I go to the meeting.

Inching my way around the building, I found a parking spot where my car was unlikely to wear someone else's paint home. Turning off the engine, I picked up my clipboard from the passenger seat, and stepped outside. Planning to head for the trunk where my laptop resided, I reached back to close my door, and glanced down to ensure my seatbelt was not about to be severed.

Good grief!

The eyeglass case lay in plain sight between my seat and the front door. It had to raise up off the floor in order to rest on the ridge where I found it.

Carol Martindale-Taylor

    Hopefully, no one noticed a little old gray-haired lady's hysterical laughter over some unheard joke, perpetrated by an unseen prankster she thanked out loud.

LETTER TO DAVE
OCTOBER 1 TO DECEMBER 28, 2016

Dear Dave:

Tue., Oct. 1, 2016. Thanks for help finding my extra eyeglasses today.

Fri., Oct. 21, 2016. This morning, I felt my bed sink like someone sat down on the lower left foot of the bed. You paying a visit?

Sun., Nov. 13, 2016. I forgot Nov. 6 was the anniversary of the awful day I found out you died. I guess forgetting is a good thing, right?

Sat., Nov. 19, 2016. Okay, was that tap on my head around 4:00 a.m. this morning the equivalent to "hey, dummy I'm still here"?

Sun., Dec. 11, 2016. Once again, there are lots of Christmas TV ads about guys buying engagement rings, and they still bother me. It is not the money, but the idea that a man cared enough to invest in one.

Then a few days ago, my mother gave me the birthstone ring Dad bought for her 40th birthday. I just realized it looks like a

Carol Martindale-Taylor

diamond engagement ring!

    Wed., Dec. 28, 2016. Does the cat ever see you? Sometimes she watches over my right shoulder, which makes me wonder.

    Love,
    Carol

A DISAPPEARING ACT

It all started back when Alan called for an API dinner meeting on April 11, in 2015. Something of an annual event by that time, this one took place to officially turn everything over to our new Team Leaders.

With no pending investigations at that time however, before long, we experienced withdrawal symptoms. It happens to dedicated paranormal investigators.

When we finally did get a client, we were more than ready to jump back into the unknown. On July 14, I dove head-first into my research mode.

Well, better get busy. I need to get this done so everybody has time to read it.

I settled down for a long session on my computer.

Okay, my API folder is under Documents.

Click.

Hum, I thought that's where I kept it. Maybe it's in this folder.

Click.

Not there either. Maybe I accidentally dumped it here.

Click, click.

I need a drink.

Walking into the kitchen, the best I could find was a can of warm Coke. Grabbing it, I headed back to my room.

Where can that thing be?

Thirty minutes later, I was completely frustrated.

I quit. It's gone. All those files from years of investigations are gone. Damn it! I must have screwed up and deleted the whole friggin' folder.

After mourning the loss of my data and reference material, I created a new file folder populated solely by this one new investigation.

Seven months passed before I needed that 'new' folder again. Given the long stretch between investigations, we were more than excited about another case, and anxious to get out into the field.

Late one night, I sat down to do my standard research for the upcoming investigation.

Let's see, that new folder is here.

Click.

Oh, give me a break. Okay, it has to be here.

Click.

Nope. Where is it?

Running through an assortment of folders and files, including places where it should never be found, produced nothing. My API folder had disappeared again.

What is this? Well, at least not much was lost this time.

Dumbfounded over my repeated mistakes, I created a third folder and saved my research in it. That folder would not be needed again for over a year.

On March 31, 2017, I looked for the twice reincarnated folder. It was gone.

Now what am I supposed to think? Were all three losses accidents? Not hardly. Is Dave or the Universe trying to tell me something?

Deciding on a test, i created a separate empty folder to see if it too disappeared.

I looked for the test folder on April 8, 2017, and discovered nothing happened to it. To this day, that folder still exists—and all three real API folders are missing.

Was I given a warning or advice? The frequency of API investigations did dwindle down, and are now a rarity.

LETTER TO DAVE
JANUARY 27 TO APRIL 20, 2017

Dear Dave:

Fri., Jan. 27, 2017. My mother brought you up again, about how my life would have been 'normal' if we had gotten married.

Sun., Feb. 19, 2017. While looking for information on the internet yesterday, up popped a Google map with Milledgeville, GA, listed. I wondered if something happened to your sister, so I sent her an e-mail about my memoir. I am never sure how she feels about all this.

Mon., Feb. 20, 2017. If we had gotten married, maybe I would not have experienced the things I have in this lifetime. Did all this help my soul advance? I am not sure. I hate to think your death and the time you spent here were wasted.

Tue., Feb. 21, 2017. I guess there really is much I may not have learned had we gotten married, but did it help my spiritual growth? I have no idea.

Wed., Mar. 1, 2017. Maybe you did send me that message about Milledgeville. Your sister fell and split her head open

Carol Martindale-Taylor

while on vacation, but she is okay.

Thu., Mar. 9, 2017. If I experienced spiritual growth during your physical absence, maybe it means your mission here is finished and you will leave. Am I supposed to thank you for leaving me all those years ago? Fat chance!

Wed., Apr. 19, 2017. A psychic medium on TV talked with clients about their survivor's guilt, and how their deceased boyfriends' spirits will always watch over them. Pure relief!
If you cannot make it for my birthday tomorrow, I will pretend you did, and will be okay with it.

Thu., Apr. 20, 2017. Well, pretending will have to do. Is it as I suspected; my soul grew after you left, so this is it until I cross over?
You love me. I trust you. You will do what is best.

Love,
Carol

A NORMAL LIFE

"What do you think your life would have been like if Dave had lived, and you two had gotten married?"

"Huh?" I glanced at my mother from my usual spot on the sofa. *Where did that come from in the middle of the TV news?*

"I mean, don't you think you would have had a normal life?"

Normal?

It was two years after Dave came forward during Allyson's reading, and for some reason, Mom started thinking about him. She certainly was on his mind when he came through acknowledging her 93rd birthday and saying "hello" to her.

"Yeah, it probably would have been a lot different."

"You know, your dad and I thought you two would be engaged by Christmas."

"Well, I know I would have had an engagement ring. That's something I never had with two husbands. And he would have been a good provider. He wasn't afraid of responsibility, or taking charge of something, otherwise he would not have been the coxswain on the captain's gig."

She stared at the floor, her nodding head telling me this Q&A session was not over.

"What kind of work do you think he would have done?"

Where is this coming from?

"I don't know, maybe something with the ocean. Fishing, tour guide, something. He wanted a catamaran, so he loved being out on the water."

"Do you think you would have moved back to Georgia?"

Needing time to digest all this, I reached for the TV Guide resting in front of me, thumbing through a few pages.

"Huh? Oh, no. He wanted to live in Northern California. We both liked it up there."

"Think you would have had any children?"

Oh my God, that's it! She missed not being a grandmother.

"Yeah, but not the dozen he talked about. He loved kids, but he was too smart for that. Maybe three or four at the most. Why?"

"Oh, I was just wondering."

She went back to watching the news, no doubt still thinking about that normal life she must have wanted for me—and her.

The big question for me was whether or not we would have survived as a couple. I will never know.

He had dreams.

I was still trying to decipher what was normal.

LETTER TO DAVE
APRIL 23 TO OCTOBER 26, 2017

Dear Dave:

Sun., Apr. 23, 2017. The tears started today while thinking about losing you again, but then I heard Andy Williams sing "I Will Wait for You" on my car radio. Not only does his video focus on a Seiko wristwatch like you bought for yourself in WestPac, the song was featured in a movie filmed the year you died.

Another psychic medium's client talked about not feeling her loved ones around her anymore, and learned it means she is healing--but that our loved ones always stay with us. I guess that means I am healing. It only took 53 years.

Fri., May 26, 2017. I think about having a half-hour reading by Allyson Walsh to see if we are still connected, but then I get scared like I was the first time.

Sat., May 27, 2017. I am not missing the physical you as much as I miss the spirit you now. However, I worry I am doing something to cut you off from me.

Sat., July 15, 2017. Mom saw Dad in her bedroom a few nights ago, and is sure about what it means for her.

Fri., July 21, 2017. I hope I can help one of our seniors at the center find peace. She is miserable about her friend's death, but does not believe in spirits, even though strange things are now happening in their house.

Thu., Sept. 7, 2017. For some reason, I would like to go back to your grave, even though you are not there. Maybe it is because I am at the end of my own life.

Fri., Oct. 20, 2017. Mom had a stroke Monday morning and is in bad shape. Her mind is still there, and that has to be horrible. Her dying does not bother me as much as watching her suffer, especially when trying to explain something she sees and she cannot do it. Thankfully, I know what she wants done—and not done—now that she is at the end of her life.

Wed., Oct. 25, 2017. I realized Mom saw Dad last week right after she was admitted to the hospital. She pointed to a blank space near the ceiling, and when I asked if she wanted to write it down, she shook her head 'yes,' but she was unable to write. I hope seeing him is helping her get through this.

Thu., Oct. 26, 2017. Mom died shortly before 2:00 p.m. today, and I was with her. She is in a better place now. She was so depressed the last year and a half that she was miserable most of the time. I bet you and Dad are with her.

Love,
Carol

GOODBYE?

It was Friday morning, November 3, 2017. The telephone rang at exactly 8:00 a.m.
Surely my boss wouldn't be calling me. I'll be there in a few minutes.

Without putting the finishing touches on my eyebrow, I sat everything down on the bathroom counter top. Forever leery of calls from Ray, I lightly walked toward the telephone in the living room, listening for the caller's voice.

After hearing my voice recording give the standard "please leave a message," the recorder kicked in.

Brrr...ring. Brrr...ring. Brrr...ring.

Ten times.

That's weird. It sounds like another telephone ringing at the other end.

I hit the button to delete the pointless recording. There was no recording.

Hum, a malfunction of some kind.

Returning to the bathroom, I reached for my eyebrow brush.
Brrr...ring. Brrr...ring. Brrr...ring.

The recorder ran during four or five rings of a telephone ringing at the other end again, and again, there was no recording of the call.

Now what's this about?

Back to the bathroom. This time, I finished the eyebrow before the phone rang again. I disconnected the call after the second ring, and as expected, there was no recording.

Now that was strange.

Shoving it to the back of my mind, I finished dressing and headed off to work.

That night, all I thought about was not feeling Dave around me anymore and how much I needed him.

Well, at least Mom is with Dad now, so she's a lot happier. Are you with them or off somewhere else?

Sitting on the sofa the following Tuesday night, I felt Dave was there, but the sensation was not as strong as in months past. I suspected it was just wishful thinking.

Then I had a passing thought.

Was that Mom ringing the phone a few mornings ago?

Some days I am slower than others. This time, it took a weekend for the significance of three separate telephone calls to get through to me.

Mom, Dad and you? Are the three of you together, and you're letting me know you're all okay? I mean, messing with a phone is so like you.

I filed the idea away with my other doubts, and concentrated on preparing for Costa Rica. I needed U.S. documents processed, and airline reservations made for a visit.

In between all this, I also needed a car rental for a quick trip to visit Delonte. I worried about leaving him.

At least he understands that when my job phases out in February, I can't live in this country on just my Social Security. No one hires 75-year-old secretaries.

***

The following Thursday when I picked up my mail, I cussed to myself over the ripped corner of my Defenders of Wildlife magazine. Turning back toward my car, a pin-point of glare caught my eye.

Why is my porch light on?

Walking into the living room, I checked the wall switch. It had been flipped on, but as has been my practice for years, I never used that light. I called the landlord.

"Hey, my porch light was on when I came home. Were any of the maintenance guys here today?"

"Nope, no one has been anywhere near there today."

I heard "she probably forgot and left it on," coming from the background in the office. Thanking the landlord, I hung up the phone.

It did not take long this time. Another light—this one in my head—beamed.

The same thing happened nine years ago, and I blew it off as something following me home from an API investigation.

This time felt like goodbye, and don't worry. We're okay, and all three of us are watching over you.

LETTER TO DAVE
JANUARY 11 TO JUNE 10, 2018

Dear Dave:

Thu., Jan. 11, 2018. It dawned on me that Cliff, Ray and Delonte all loved me, but it was a love born out of need. You just loved me.

Fri., Jan. 26, 2018. The prison did something about Delonte's health; a CT scan (after I called the warden's office). No colonoscopy though, and we have been asking for one since May of last year.

Fri., Mar. 30, 2018. I spent March 2 to 7 in Costa Rica; beautiful place, friendly people, and scary not being proficient in Spanish.

On my flight from Dallas to Costa Rica, we had mechanical problems and circled Dallas using up fuel until it was safe to land. I was not scared—how is that for faith that if it was the end, I would see you?

Mon., Apr. 16, 2018. I drove to Maryland to visit Delonte over April 6 and 7. He has given up on getting out, and does not even realize it. After all these years, his arms, chest and neck are now covered in tattoos that include my name and initials.

I believe turning on that porch light last November was your way of telling me your mission is over. Thank you so much for helping me heal.

I did send Allyson Walsh an e-mail though, asking what she thinks about you coming through in a reading again.

Sun., Apr. 29, 2018. I arrived in Grecia, Costa Rica, one week ago today, and it is beautiful.

My instincts are correct; Allyson said you are not around me. She said I should wait until I am settled, and then "see what happens."

I love you, wherever the hell you are.

Sun., June 10, 2018. Is there anything you can do to help Delonte find another woman? Even if I keep sending him money, at least I would not have the emotional ties. I guess this will end eventually. Either I will drop dead or he will, and that will be that.

Love,
Carol

DOUBTS

Feeling settled enough in Costa Rica by the end of June to start writing again, I returned to my research for a future book.

A fictional story set in 1898, it includes a hot-headed Gypsy violinist from Romania, who settles down in Hungary for an extended period of time. A key player in the story, his character development necessitated researching traditional Gypsy music.

One afternoon, with cell phone charged and ready, note pad and pen at my side, I pulled up Google. Keying in 'compare Hungarian Gypsy music to Romanian Gypsy music,' multiple sites appeared. As it happens, there is a difference between the two styles.

Guess I better listen to some samples so I sound like I know what I'm talking about.

I clicked on samples shown at the very top of the list.

Hum, those Romanian pieces do have a different cadence than the Hungarian pieces.

A few handwritten notes later, I decided to play it safe.

I better listen to a few more samples to make sure I'm picking up on the right thing.

I glanced down at my cell phone screen to click on the next selection.

'I Will Wait for You.'

What?

Wait a minute. It's by Andy Williams and some female singer I've never heard of—maybe she's a Gypsy.
Nope, doesn't look like it.
Maybe the movie featuring the song was about a Gypsy.
Nope, doesn't appear so.
I could find no reason why 'I Will Wait for You' appeared on my phone.
Did you come through electronically? If it was you, thank you so much!
I could not resist messaging Allyson Walsh, and she responded with an interesting comment. Yes, I could be causing Dave's absence. If we living folks are involved in something requiring serious concentration, we can pull our own energy away, and spirits cannot get through.
Did I cause Dave to pull back, or was it just time for him to do so? Did he come through because I am more relaxed now? I do know I worried about exactly that happening as far back as May of 2017.
Then my usual doubts started. Analyzing, days of analyzing, but by the end of the month, I came full circle.
I think you did communicate with me by using 'I Will Wait for You.' Why else would it have appeared?
Will I ever stop doubting?

LETTER TO DAVE
JUNE 28 TO OCTOBER 20, 2018

Dear Dave:

Thu., June 28, 2018. There was no reason for the song 'I Will Wait for You' to appear on my cell phone. I could not resist telling Allyson, and she said we can divert our energy and block out spirits. I did not mean for that to happen.

Sat., Sept. 8, 2018. Delonte has had a bad time with his health lately, but they say he does not have cancer, although he still needs surgery.

Sun., Sept. 23, 2018. Things went to hell in a hurry. After one year of Delonte's GI-tract symptoms being ignored, non-prison doctors could not save him. When I arrived on Sept. 13, he glanced at me as I walked into his hospital room, and he never looked at me again. A single tear rolled down his cheek. He died on Sept. 17, from a cancerous duodenal mass.

Still no tears of my own. I feel terrible, but I also feel relief. He suffered so much all his adult life for such a small part in the crime landing him in prison, but now he is free.

So am I.

Fri., Oct. 19, 2018. A copy of your files mixed in with Delonte's on my computer recently, a black and white butterfly visited for several minutes, a brown feather appeared on my patio and a white feather appeared next to my kitchen stove. I told Delonte he better find ways to let me know he is okay!

Are you two together? Are you helping him adjust on your side? You know I loved him in one way, but I love you in another, one that transcends this lifetime.

You are my home.

Sat., Oct, 20, 2018. No parents, no siblings, no husband and no physical you. While starting this final chapter in my life however, I believe you and my parents are watching over me.

Love,
Carol

DEAR DAVE

You knew I was in trouble. Night after night, in front of my computer beginning in late 2013, I watched pictures of you pop up on the monitor. I relived every detail and struggled to understand why you died. As the weeks rolled by, my despair deepened, and after all these years, the tears flowed.

Fifty years passed before I attempted writing about you, then in a mere five minutes late one night, I realized how my entire life shifted after you left. Survivor's guilt moved in sometime during 1964, and I allowed it to take control. I did not save you, so I tried saving other men. Now I know you were not meant to be saved.

Perhaps our story of love crossing over between two worlds will help others grieving for lost loved ones as they travel their own path of discovery. Maybe we can prevent a survivor of such tragedy from compounding the trauma, and help them move on with the knowledge that their loss is not permanent.

Yet there is something else to consider. Some psychics and psychic researchers believe spirits plan life's lessons before incarnating in order to facilitate a soul's growth. This may mean one person returns to the spirit world, leaving loved ones behind to gain more insight. These plans are not made in a vacuum, but through discussions in groups of souls comprised of spirit friends.

This is not to say there is no such thing as free will. It is suggested that there are multiple roads available to us, but the one chosen is a decision we make as incarnate individuals.

According to this premise, you and I agreed you would leave here early to help my soul grow. Both a professional and a non-professional psychic medium said you have been on a mission, and stayed here to help my soul develop. Both spoke of your sheer will power and determination to stay with me.

If this is true, I need to compare our probable lifestyle had we married, against what I have actually done over these last 50 years. Being exposed to the world does not mean learning from it.

I believe you would have been a good provider. You were intelligent, and as shown by your duty assignment on the *USS Mahan,* not afraid of responsibility. That translates into an unwillingness to allow me to be the primary bread winner in the family, a position I maintained throughout both of my marriages.

There certainly would have been some of those babies you wanted. You were too smart to father the dozen you often laughed about, but there would have been children. That said, although I might have continued working outside the home, my life would have been devoted to you and raising our children.

We would likely have lived in Northern California in a pre-dominantly White neighborhood, probably offering limited exposure to other races and cultures.

As a family, we may have taken vacations, attended school activities, and had a circle of like-minded friends. We would certainly have made trips to Georgia to visit your family, just as they may have visited us.

There would have been our share of problems. We never gave each other grief over previous relationships, or put pressure on each other about dating or sex. However, I doubt I was strong enough to deal with other women flirting with you, as often happened. I could have made your life hell.

I have had my share of men attempt to enter my life. How

would you have dealt with them? Would the apparent temper that flared up in your fight on the *Mahan* have exacted its toll on our marriage?

There would have been the usual disagreements couples have over finances and raising children. We may not even have survived as a family.

In other words, it would have been the normal life my mother mentioned when talking about us as a couple.

Instead, you died.

Left to my own devices for five decades, my roots spread from the Midwest, to the West Coast, East Coast, Southwest, Southern Plains and Costa Rica. En route, I completed a bachelor's degree in anthropology and a master's degree in criminal justice.

I met and worked with people of all races, ethnicities and religions, finding they have the same hopes and dreams, yet different opinions. I loved two men from races other than my own. I like to think I learned from them all.

Outside interests landed me in political marches in Washington, D.C., working on prison reform, lobbying Congress on Mexican wolf reintroduction and digging in the dirt as an amateur archaeologist.

So how much of this life style would have injected itself into our marriage? Probably not much.

If the intent of all this was to instruct my soul, I hope it worked. I hate to think you wasted your time hanging around here.

Then came paranormal investigating.

While working on many cases over my first seven years as a paranormal investigator, I believed my interest in the Other Side began early in life, and that while others experienced the presence of deceased loved ones, I did not.

Then one casual Sunday afternoon in July of 2014, my cell phone started ringing while it was turned off. Had you not been able to do that, I would still be looking for 'logical' explanations for everything going on around me. Maybe someday you will show me how such things are done.

So here I am now. You can be with me, and apparently have been for some time. Sometimes I think I am dreaming, then I feel so loved, I am certain you are nearby. You have clearly given me signs you are here, and all I can do is thank you.

I made your death my own in some ways, and when that naive Carol left with you, she opened a door for men perceived to be in need of saving. I tried, because after all, I failed to save you.

Over the years, I discovered it could not be done. I only hope I fulfilled my role for them as they walked their own journey, just as you and I have walked ours.

Maybe my road was planned as a learning experience, and completion of this memoir, my destination. Maybe not. Regardless, I hope some find comfort in reading our story, and that it prevents them from falling into a life-time pattern of feeding their survivor's guilt. May they at least be open to the idea that the spirits of our loved ones stay with us until we are together again.

However, if there are pre-planned paths for us to choose from, and they take one similar to mine, all bets are off. They, and their free will, are on their own.

Others will never believe our story, chalking it off as the ramblings of an old woman grasping at straws. So be it. The only advice I offer them is to please consider all options if their cell phone keeps ringing while it is turned off.

As for us, I know you are no longer around me as much as in the recent past. According to psychics, this happens when survivors begin the healing process. Thankfully, they also say our loved ones continue watching over us, and that our bond of love will never be broken.

Am I healing? I watch your pictures slide by on my computer now, and smile. I seldom think about the why's and how's of your death. I am healing, and thanks to you, ready to get on with what remains of my life.

I trust you completely, and know you will do whatever is best for both of us. A deep sense of peace floods over me knowing you are in the here and now, but more than anything else,

Carol Martindale-Taylor

knowing you will be there for me when I cross over.
   We certainly have a lot to talk about.

THAT IS THE QUESTION

"To be or not to be, that is the question."
In mid-2014, I began suspecting Dave's presence, and soon knew he was back in my life. But how did I circle around from that point, to wondering if he was still here, to believing he was not, and back to knowing he was present?

Steeped in my own misery every night, it never occurred to me he would pay a visit. Even when my cell phone rang twice that day while it was turned off, I assumed it was due to a previous investigation done for an API client.

Then an incident, one of those I always considered suspect when our clients talked about them, happened to me. I felt Dave's presence. No vision. No touch. I just knew he was sitting against me on my right side, exactly where he would have been in life.

From that time until shortly after my reading with Allyson Walsh, I felt him nearby. His talent for manipulating electronics confirmed I was not losing my mind.

But things cooled down. Incidents happened farther apart, and the sensation of his presence weakened. Fear of losing him twice in the same lifetime terrified me.

There were times when I thought an incident was direct contact from him, or related to him, only to discover it probably was not. No one was near a neighbor's parked car when I walked out the door one night and said aloud "Merry Christmas babe." Its lights instantly snapped on and off, and it happened again many times. Too many to be paranormal.

I later discovered a car can be locked and unlocked by its owner from some distance away, and even from inside a building. In all probability, it was mere coincidence. Oops, there is that word.

DNA results showing my ancestry as 1/3 British Isles, and our family names listed in current English telephone books, suggested we might have shared a previous life there or in Ireland. However, a recent reanalysis by Ancestry.com corrected my heritage to the one I expected—predominantly Eastern European. That poses other possible scenarios, taking me back to my past life regression session where Amelia and Isahkoff spent their lives in Eastern Europe. More questions with unknowable answers.

Other times, something happened and it took me hours or days to realize it was contact by Dave.

I continually vacillated back and forth about whether or not he was with me, and whether or not I could be a 'big girl' about it. Aside from clouding my judgment at times, it must have driven him crazy, no matter which world he was in at that moment.

As my attitude evolved, so did my struggles. Not a trained scientist, I still function within a scientific mind set, and both halves of my brain love a good argument.

One side needs hard proof. Getting excited during a paranormal investigation about a jiggling camera, energy manifesting out of thin air, or a trail of ectoplasm spreading across a scene, can be self-defeating. We usually discovered it was a cat brushing against the legs of a tripod, our own breath exhaled into frigid night air, or a spider's web draping itself across a camera lens.

Sounds can be deceiving. Hot water heaters crackling, kids playing in the hallway, even neighbors talking down the block, can skew voice recordings. They need to be sorted out with caution.

After excluding the regular sights and sounds of daily living, then you can start delving into other possibilities. Those possibilities have their own issues if they are not recorded. Personal experiences that cannot be verified leave the witness explaining they are not crazy or unbelievably gullible to people who believe they truly are crazy or unbelievably gullible.

The other side of my brain believes that thousands of research projects, and millions of consistent world-wide experiences, mean the Other Side exists. I do not have to see it. My own logic tells me the millions of people experiencing such things are not all ignorant, or in collusion with each other. Long before mass communication, people in every culture around the world had such experiences.

So my problem is locked somewhere between those two arguments. I believe in the paranormal experiences of others, but when it comes to my own, I need solid proof. I certainly never believed anything like this would happen to me.

Enter Dave. Whatever happens now is up to him and the Universe, however they work.

I trust him completely, and believe he will be waiting for me when I cross over...but I still plan to give him hell.

THE NOW

All my adult life, I thought of myself as a relatively strong woman doing my own thing. I am not afraid to be alone, travel alone or move across country—and internationally— alone. Like many others, I have survived the passing of parents, a husband and other loved ones.

I also survived the tragic death of a young man named James David Alligood.

In 2013, I decided to write the magazine article vegetating in the back of my mind for the last five decades. I expected writing about Dave's death would be good therapy, so I fought my reopened wounds while creating the sibilance of a story. Weeks later, I re-read the manuscript late one night.

My epiphany went something like *you dumb little shit, that's what you've done!*

I knew about survivor's guilt. It makes sense, and my heart went out to those dealing with it. But me? No, I am that strong woman who dealt with his loss on my own, and hey, look at me now.

Except...well, why was I drawn to Dave, strong and independent at a young age, yet the three main men in my later life were all insecure and needy?

The answer stared back at me in my own writing. Survivor's guilt told me I did not save Dave, so I needed to save other men.

But that is only part of my story. Those re-opened wounds were raw, and although I stopped the hemorrhaging in 1964, it was with a Band-Aid. In writing about his death, I discovered the original wounds were never flushed out and properly healed. The bleeding started in earnest.

Night after night in tears, I studied his pictures, reliving every moment in them. I believe my depth of despair drew him out into the open. As one psychic stated, "he was on a mission," and another talked of the "magnetic pull" between us.

I spent a lot of time arguing with myself. Is my imagination working overtime? How much can I accept on face value? What should I dismiss? Is this real? Am I truly experiencing the paranormal?

Merriam-Webster defines the paranormal as that which is not scientifically explainable. Do I present hard science one way or the other? No. What I do present is a series of incidents occurring between July of 2014 and October of 2018, some of which were recorded, and some of which cannot be explained. Make of them what you will.

As an experienced paranormal investigator, and one with a reputation for de-bunking suspicious phenomena, I never anticipated psychic experiences in my own life. During my first seven years with API, I assumed such things happened only to our clients.

Then my cell phone rang not once, but twice while it was turned off. Based on the experiences of our clients and API team members, I assumed someone followed me home from an investigation. The rest is history as they say, and I cannot thank Dave enough for not giving up on me.

Now I understand why I did certain things and loved certain men, giving me a new appreciation for them. My life with Dave does not take anything away from them and what we felt for each other.

Today, I worry about loved ones left behind who grieve for the rest of their lives. Finding themselves affected by their loss each and every day, they struggle to carry on with life. To them, I can only say miss your loved one, cherish what you had together, and know they will be with you forever. Yes, we have lost that physical contact we crave, but if the psychics are only partially correct, those we love are awaiting for us on the Other Side. Their love for us transcends the physical.

After all I experienced before and after Dave's death, I can truly say the happiest moment in my entire life was hearing Allyson Walsh say "he says he'll be there for you when you come over." I believe he loves me from wherever he is, and that he will watch over me until it is my time to leave here.

Through all my indecision and doubts, there is one thing about which I am absolutely certain. Dave is waiting for me.

In the meantime, I never imagined laughing with him again.

AFTERWARD

Memories are strange things. Some decades old remain as vivid as this morning's piping hot coffee, while others cool immediately. This memoir captures my past as I recall it, but if you recognize yourself in it, and see variations between what we remember, please accept my apology. Memories are indeed slippery beings.

I changed the names of a few to preserve their privacy as unwilling participants, but real names are given as well. I hope those who see their names in print approve. Knowing what I know now, I offer the same explanation to those on the Other Side.

In chapters with letters to Dave, and in some conversations, I paraphrased the wording to avoid the repetition and rambling of personal conversations. In all cases, the intent was left intact.

My thanks must go out to those who contributed to my life, as well as those who contributed to the publication of this book.

To my parents, Frank and Emily Berhar, thank you for the solid foundation on which I have survived until today. I know you both continue to watch over me.

To the Alligood family, all I can say is thank you for allowing me the privilege of knowing Dave, then and now.

Alice Kisor Powers, Bob Powers and Johnny Adkins—what would I have done without you during the worst tragedy of my life?

A big 'thank you' goes to Alan Silva and the Arkansas Paranormal Investigations team—Myrna Coyle, Beckie Moore, and Jeff and Michelle Young. What enlightening times we shared for so many good years.

None of this would have been possible without the help of other writers, both professionals and those who write for writing's sake. My college professors, Tony Hillerman and Norman Zollinger inspired me, and the solid advice from Alison Taylor-Brown and other writers associated with the Village Writing School in Arkansas, proved instrumental in completing this project.

Psychic medium Allyson Walsh not only confirmed what was happening in my life, but kept my feet on the ground.

As always, friends sustain us when they are non-judgmental sounding boards. The brief time with Jan Holzle, and long-time friendships with Lorraine Heartfield, Joan Glassell, Laural Ward and Josephine Tester helped me through a time when I often questioned my sanity. Thank you all.

An extra thank you must go to Laurel Ward, Lorraine Heartfield and Michelle Teague for their help as beta readers, Alison Taylor-Brown for her 'unofficial' editing, and Cynthia Gilmore for her proof-reading skills. Their review and input certainly guided me in this effort.

I hope readers use my experience to prevent their own survivor's guilt from ruling their lives. I also hope non-believers in the paranormal open themselves up, if just a little, to the possibilities offered to us from the Other Side.

For the rest of us, the believers, what pure joy we know!

ABOUT THE AUTHOR

Born in Chicago and raised in the small town of Norwalk, IA, I eventually lived on both Coasts, in the Southwest, the Southern Plains and now Costa Rica. Travel is truly the great educator.

While earning my bachelor's and master's degrees late in life, I also became involved in environmental issues, prison reform, archaeology and paranormal investigating. My planned series of historical fiction books will draw from this background, and you may follow my progress at: www.carolmartindale.wordpress.com.

Thank you for reading my book, and please know that your review is appreciated!